CIVIL WAR REGIMENTS

FROM

MAINE

JOSHUA LAWRENCE CHAMBERLAIN

eBooksOnDisk.com
2003

Orginially Published in 1908
by the
Federal Publishing Company

CONTENTS

OTHER PAPERBACK TITLES FROM EBOOKSONDISK

Civil War Regiments from Wisconsin by Jerome A. Watrous.
ISBN 1932157115

Civil War Regiments from New Jersey by James Stewert, Jr.
ISBN 1932157239

Civil War Regiments from Massachusetts by Francis Agustus Osborn
ISBN 1932157212

Confederate Military History of Alabama by Joseph Wheeler.
ISBN 1932157174

Confederate Military History of Florida by J. J. Dickison.
ISBN 1932157093

Confederate Military History of Mississippi by Charles E. Hooker.
ISBN 1932157182

Confederate Military History of Texas by Oran M. Robert.
ISBN 193215714X

Regimental Losses in the American Civil War by William F. Fox
1932157077

CIVIL WAR REGIMENTS

FROM

MAINE

JOSHUA L. CHAMBERLAIN

JOSHUA L. Chamberlain, major-general, was born in Brewer, Me., Sept. 8, 1828. His father proposed an army career for him, and sent him at the age of fourteen to the military academy of Maj. Whiting at Ellsworth, Me., where one lasting benefit was the compulsory acquirement of some practical acquaintance with the French language. After some time spent in that institution of learning, and in teaching country school and other remunerative employment, he decided to become a minister of the gospel; and finally, having committed to memory Kuhner's unabridged Greek grammar from alphabet to appendix, he entered Bowdoin college with advanced standing at the age of nineteen. Graduating at the college in 1852, he entered Bangor theological seminary, where, besides conforming to all regulations, he read his theology in Latin and his church history in German, and took up the study of the Hebrew, Syriac and Arabic languages, to which he continued to devote not less than an hour a day for six years. Before his graduation, having written the four sermons required, and occasionally preached them, he received "calls" from three important churches; but the remarkable impression made by his "Master's Oration" at Bowdoin in 1855 on "Law and Liberty" led to his immediate appointment as instructor in the department of natural and revealed religion. The next year he was elected professor of rhetoric and oratory and held this place for five years. In July, 1862, leave of absence for two years was granted him for the purpose of pursuing his studies in Europe, but the serious reverses of the Union army and the critical condition of the country at that time seemed to him a call to service in another field. On Aug. 8 he was made lieutenant-colonel of the 20th regiment of Maine volunteers. In twenty days he had the organization complete with full ranks, turned the command over to Col. Ames of the regular army, and set forth for the field. The regiment was assigned to Butterfield's division, Porter's corps, Army of the Potomac. Col. Chamberlain's qualities were tested in the sharp engagement at Shepherdstown ford immediately after the battle of Antietam, in September, and in the terrible experiences of his command in the disastrous battle of

1

Fredericksburg in December he certainly won the master's degree in his military education. He had an arduous part in all the trying operations of that winter on the Rappahannock. In May, 1863, he was made colonel of his regiment, having already acted in that capacity for three months. At Gettysburg, July 2, he held the extreme left of the Union line, and his conduct on that occasion in the memorable defense of Little Round Top won for him the admiration of the army and public fame, and he was recognized by the government in the bestowal of the Congressional medal of honor for "conspicuous personal gallantry and distinguished service." He was immediately placed in command of the famous "light brigade" of the division, which he handled with marked skill in the action at Rappahannock station. At Spottsylvania Court House in May, 1864, he was placed in command of a "forlorn hope" of nine picked regiments to make a night assault on a hitherto impregnable point of the enemy's works. By remarkable judgment and skill he gained the position, but in the morning it was found to be commanded on both flanks by the enemy in force, therefore utterly untenable, and the withdrawal ordered was more difficult than the advance had been. Shortly afterward came the sharp engagements on the Totopotomy and the North Anna, and the terrible battles of Bethesda Church and Cold Harbor, in all of which his coolness of judgment and quickness of action drew special commendation. He was promoted to colonel of the 20th Maine on May 18, as stated above, and one month later, in command of a brigade, he made the desperate charge on Rives' salient in the Petersburg lines, where Gen. Grant promoted him on the field to the rank of brigadier-general "for gallant conduct in leading his brigade against a superior force of the enemy and for meritorious service" in that terrible campaign of 1864. In this assault he was seriously wounded and reported dead, but after two months of intense suffering he returned to his command. In the last campaign of the war, with two brigades he led the advance of the infantry with Sheridan, and made the brilliant opening fight on the Quaker road, March 29, 1865, where he was twice wounded (in the left arm and breast), and his horse was shot under him. His conduct again drew attention of the government, and he was promoted to the brevet rank of major-general "for conspicuous gallantry" in this action. On the White Oak road, March 31, although much disabled by wounds, he distinguished himself

2

by recovering a lost field; and in the battle of Five Forks, April 1, his promptitude and skillful handling of troops received special official mention. In the final action at Appomattox Court House, April 9, he was called by Gen. Sheridan to replace his leading division of cavalry, and the first flag of truce from Longstreet came to him. His corps commander says in an official report: "In the final action Gen. Chamberlain had the advance, and was driving the enemy rapidly before him when the announcement of the surrender was made." At the formal surrender of Lee's army he was designated to command the parade before which that army laid down the arms and colors of the Confederacy. At the final grand review in Washington, his division had the honor of being placed at the head of the column of the Army of the Potomac, and his troops, fresh from the surrender at Appomattox, were received by the thronging spectators as might be imagined. In the reorganization of the regular army at the close of hostilities he was offered a colonelcy, with the privilege of retiring with the rank of brigadier-general, on account of wounds received in the service. Not caring to be a soldier in time of peace, he declined this offer, and was mustered out of military service Jan. 15, 1866. Returning to Maine he was offered the choice of several diplomatic offices abroad, but almost as soon as he was out of the army, he was elected governor of the state by the largest majority ever given in that commonwealth. His administration was very satisfactory and he was continued in that office for four terms. While popular with the people he was in some disfavor with his party because he did not approve the policy of conferring the privilege of the "suffrage" on the lately liberated slaves, holding that reconstruction could only be effected by and through the best minds of the south, a position that history has thoroughly vindicated. In 1871 Gen. Chamberlain was elected president of Bowdoin college, and held that position until 1883, when he resigned, although continuing to lecture on public law and public economy until 1885. He was appointed major-general of Maine militia in 1876, was United States commissioner to the Paris exposition in 1878, and in 1885 he went to Florida as president of a railroad construction company. In 1900 he was appointed by President McKinley surveyor of customs at the port of Portland, and is still the efficient occupant of that position. Thus it will be seen that Gen. Chamberlain is still an active man of affairs. He is in great request as a speaker on public occasions and as a writer

3

he has an extended reputation. He has recently been engaged in writing out his notes on the last campaign of the Army of the Potomac, which he contemplates publishing under the title, "The Passing of the Armies: Last Campaign of Grant and Lee." He also revised and edited the manuscript pertaining to the state military history of Maine, which appears as a part of this publication.

Military Affairs in Maine
1861—65

NO one of the loyal states can claim preeminence over the Pine Tree State in its conduct during the Civil war. The universal sentiment of her people was that the Union must be preserved and the supremacy of the law maintained at whatever cost of life and treasure. All the patriotism of their revolutionary ancestors showed forth in the prompt and energetic action taken by her citizens in support of the general government, and in the determination that our institutions should be preserved as handed down by the fathers. The excess of her devotion to the Union, and some of her enormous sacrifices in blood and treasure will be briefly recorded in the following pages. Unnumbered pages would not suffice to tell in detail the splendid history of individual sacrifice and heroism on the part of her citizens during the continuance of the great struggle for the life of the nation.

The distant mutterings of rebellion had been heard for many months, and four of the Southern States had already passed ordinances of secession, while several others were threatening to pass similar ordinances, when the legislature of the State of Maine took steps to assure the government at Washington of its unswerving loyalty, and passed on Jan. 16, 1861, by a large majority, the following joint resolutions:—"Whereas, By advices received from Washington, and by information received in many other ways, it appears that an extensive combination exists of evil-disposed persons to effect the dissolution of the Federal Union, and the overthrow of the Government ; and whereas the people of the state are deeply attached to the Union and thoroughly loyal to the government, and are heartily devoted to their preservation and protection; therefore, "Resolved, That the governor be, and hereby is, authorized and requested to assure the president of the United States of the loyalty of the people of Maine to the Union and the government thereof; and that the entire resources of the state in men and money are hereby pledged to the administration in defence and support of the Constitution and the Union."

When the news reached the people of Maine that the first gun of rebellion had been fired upon our national flag, and that the United States fort, Sumter, in Charleston Harbor, S. C., had been assaulted and reduced, April 12, 1861, a great wave of patriotic ardor swept over the whole state. Everywhere her sons and daughters were inspired by a spirit of determination to avenge the blow that had been struck, and to aid the government in crushing the treasonable movement. Men forgot their party affiliations, and patriotic assemblages gathered in all the principal places in the state to voice their undying devotion to the Union. All were animated by the same spirit of sacrifice, and active steps were at once taken to form military organizations. The hills and valleys of Maine resounded with martial music and the gleam of bristling bayonets was seen throughout the land. In some towns, in less than twenty-four hours, full companies of volunteers were formed, ready to march. The pulpit and the press united in the demand that the state should do its full share in upholding the government. Banks and private citizens hastened to tender such material aid to the government for war purposes as might be found essential. Mr. Henry B. Humphrey, a wealthy gentleman of Thomaston, offered to arm and equip a company of artillery at an expense of $15,000. Mothers, wives and sisters were animated by the same loyal spirit, and some of the women of Skowhegan, eager to testify their devotion to the nation, got out a field piece and fired a salute of 34 guns. The first companies to tender their services were the Lewiston Light Infantry, Auburn Artillery, and Portland Rifle Guards. The first named organization was the first to fill its ranks and be accepted and ordered into service by the governor. In Cherryfield, four hours after the enlistment roll was opened, fifty volunteers had entered their names. A poll of a volunteer company in China on the question of an immediate tender of their services to the state, showed no dissenting voice. Many other towns acted with almost equal zeal and promptitude.

The long reign of peace had rendered military organizations unnecessary, and the opening of hostilities found the militia of Maine in a neglected and unprepared condition. There was an enrolled but unarmed militia of about 60,000 men, and not more than 1,200 of these were in a condition to respond to any sudden call to arms in the emergencies contemplated by the constitution of the state. Nevertheless, within two weeks of the president's call for 75,000 volunteers, April 15, 1861, the 1st regiment of infantry was organized under the command of the gallant Nathaniel J. Jackson of Lewiston, and in less than a month the 2nd regiment was also ready for service, commanded by the brave and lamented Charles D. Jameson of Bangor. Sickness somewhat delayed the departure of the 1st regiment from the state, and the 2nd was the first to start for the seat of war, armed and equipped so well that it received the warm encomiums of Mr. Cameron, the secretary of war.

Maine was most fortunate in having, from the commencement of the war, able and incorruptible chief magistrates, imbued with the loftiest patriotism, and whose great ambition was to furnish men and means for the suppression of the rebellion as promptly and economically as it was possible to do. At the outbreak of hostilities, Israel Washburn, Jr., was in the gubernatorial chair, and labored under almost insurmountable difficulties in his efforts to organize an effective military force from the crude and chaotic elements of the state militia system. He found himself without sufficient authority of law to meet the requisition made, on him by the president for a portion of the state militia to be used in suppressing the armed uprising against the Federal government, and on April 16, the day following President Lincoln's first call for troops, he called the legislature in extra session, to convene on the 22nd. He used this language in his proclamation summoning the law-making body:—"The fact that the laws of the United States have been, and now are opposed, and their execution obstructed, in the States of South Carolina, Georgia, Alabama, Florida, Mississippi, Louisiana and Texas, by a combination too powerful to be suppressed by the ordinary course of judicial proceedings, or by the power vested in the marshals by the laws that are; the fact that a requisition has been made on me by the President of the United States for a portion of the militia of the state to aid in suppressing such combinations, and causing the laws to be duly executed; the fact that I find myself without sufficient authority of law to enable me to respond thereto as the exigency of the case requires,—these facts present in my judgment, one of those extraordinary occasions contemplated in the constitution for the convening of the legislature. In consideration whereof, I, Israel Washburn, Jr., governor of the State of Maine, in virtue of the power vested in me by the constitution to convene the legislature of this state, hereby require the senators and representatives to assemble in their respective chambers at the capitol in Augusta, on Monday, the 22nd day of April instant, at 12 o'clock noon, and then and there to consider and determine on such measures as the condition of the country and the obligation of the state may seem to demand."

The legislature sat for only three and a half days, but during that time, enacted with commendable promptness and unanimity all laws necessary to enable the state to do its share in meeting the remarkable crisis of the country. An act was passed to receive, arm, and equip ten regiments of volunteers, not to exceed 10,000 men, and authorizing a loan of $1,000,000 to meet this expense. A bill was also passed to raise a volunteer corps of militia of three regiments, not to exceed 3,000 men, who should be armed, equipped and drilled at the expense of the state, and subject to be called into actual service at the demand of the proper authorities. The volunteers in actual service were to receive two months bounty and the regular pay of $11 per month. Steps were also taken to place the whole militia force of the state in the most effective condition. The governor was authorized, if in his discretion the public safety should demand it, to make provision for the organization of coast guards to protect the commerce and harbors of the state from privateers. It authorized a loan of $300,000, in case it was deemed necessary to provide this coast guard. This prompt and patriotic action of the legislature influenced all classes. The ship-builders and shipowners of the state met and offered their vessels to the government; lumbermen, fishermen, and men of all professions hastened to volunteer their services in the companies which were now being rapidly formed. A general order was at once promulgated calling for 10,000 volunteers, to be organized into ten regiments, without regard to military districts, to be immediately enlisted and mustered into the active militia service of the State.

Strange as it may now seem, the general government believed that the rebellion would be quickly repressed, and the original call for troops on April 15, was for only three months service. The legislative act authorizing these troops to be raised in Maine, caused them to be enlisted for two years unless sooner discharged, and the 1st and 2nd regiments were so enlisted; the former was mustered into the service of the United States for three months, and the latter for two years. On May 3, 1861, the president issued another call for troops. Under this call, and under acts approved July 22 and 25, 1861, 500,000 men were required, orders were issued from the war department, requiring all state volunteers to be mustered into government service for three years. Meanwhile the 3d, 4th, 5th and 6th regiments had been organized and enlisted for two years under the above mentioned act of the legislature, when the three years requirement was issued from Washington, which necessitated an amendment in the state's mode of enlistment. The men in the four regiments above mentioned were asked to sign a contract to serve for an additional year, and those who declined, with the exception of the 1st and 2nd regiments, were discharged.

Such was the zeal of the patriotic citizens of the state, that within a few weeks after the adjournment of the extra session of the legislature, companies had been organized far in excess of the needs of the hour. After sending forward the first six regiments, the last of which was mustered into the service of the United States on July 15, 1861, Gov. Washburn decided to discontinue enlistments in consequence of word received from Washington that no more troops from Maine would be accepted. The following organized companies were now required to disband, or, if they preferred, be placed upon such footing as to drill and compensation, as would measurably relieve them from the sacrifices entailed in keeping up a military organization, and yet secure their services when called for:

Capt. West's, East Machias; Capt. Sawyer's, Dixmont; Capt. Roberts', Dexter; Capt. Boynton's, Newport; Capt. Carlisle's, Bangor; Capt. Cass', Bangor; Capt. Lawrence's, Gardiner; Capt. Norris', Monmouth; Capt. Duly's, Phippsburg; Capt. Jones', Waldoboro; Capt. Crowell's, Winterport; Capt. Robinson's, Unity; Capt. Jones', China; Capt. Chase's, Fairfield; Capt. McDonald's, Buckfield; Capt. Houghton's, Woodstock; Capt. McArthur's, Limington; Capt. Andrews, Biddeford. Four of these companies elected to maintain their organizations, viz.: Duly's, Jones' of Waldoboro, Robinson's and Andrews, and to devote not less than two days per week to drill and instruction until otherwise ordered, and to be paid pro rata therefor, without quarters or rations. The other companies were given leave of absence, without pay or rations, until called for. Twelve of these commanding officers, together with large portions of their commands, as then existing, subsequently entered the service of the United States in regiments which were later accepted, as was also true of Capt.

Hutchin's company, of New Portland, which was also put upon leave of absence.

About this time Brig.-Gen. Thomas W. Sherman visited the state and concerted measures with Gov. Washburn in regard to his naval expedition, when it was then learned that more regiments would be required. The work of organizing new regiments was accordingly recommenced with vigor, and four other regiments were speedily mustered into the United States service.

In the first battle of Bull Run, July 21, 1861, the troops of Maine bore an honorable and conspicuous part, and despite the reverse suffered by the Union Army of McDowell, won fame for themselves and glory for their state. Of the Federal troops actually engaged in this fight, nearly one-fourth were from Maine. This disaster to the national forces led to an order by Gov. Washburn directing the enlistment of additional regiments of volunteers. This document recited: — "Whilst observing, with the most grateful pride and admiration, the brave conduct of our regiments already in the field, the governor and commander-in-chief calls upon the loyal men of the state to emulate the patriotic zeal and courage of their brothers who have gone before them. The issue involved is one on which there can be no divided opinion in Maine. It affects not only the integrity of our Union, but the very life of republican government. For the preservation of these, Maine will pour out her best blood, and expend her richest treasure. Having already contributed generously of the flower of her youth and manhood, Maine must send yet more of her stalwart sons, to do battle for the preservation of the Union, and for the supremacy of law."

The recruiting service of the state was again in active operation from this time forward, until the general government relieved Maine from all further participation in the work early in the following year. Many of the states were ahead of Maine at this time in the quota of troops furnished the government, and were still rapidly forming new military organizations, so authority was given Maine by the war department to organize five more regiments of infantry (with power to increase the number to eight), a regiment of cavalry, six batteries of light artillery, and a company of sharpshooters. Many voluntary organizations of an informal nature for military service had been formed in various parts of the state since the outbreak of hostilities; organizations which not only took their rise without compulsion, but were maintained after repeated refusals to their applications for formal enlistment in the service of the state. Not in many years had there been seen such an array of citizen soldiery parading for discipline and review, as was to be observed in the months of September and October, 1861. Little trouble was therefore found in raising these additional troops, together with four companies of coast guards, which served by authority of the war department. All told, the State of Maine raised during the year 1861 sixteen regiments (one of them one of the best cavalry regiments in the service), six batteries of artillery, and a company of sharpshooters, besides four companies of coast guards. This was 2,500 in excess of her quota, and those regiments which had gone forward to the seat of war gloriously maintained the high reputation of the state for bravery and self-possession in the numerous battles.

The elections for state officers and members of the legislature in 1861, on the issue of the vigorous prosecution of the war, sustained the government by a majority of nearly 60,000. Arrangements were made during this year for the erection of a fort at the mouth of the Kennebec river. An appropriation of $100,000 by Congress had been made for this purpose four years earlier, but Secretary Floyd had refused to take the necessary steps for procuring a title and domain over the land necessary for its location. It is only just to say that the movement to increase the defences of the seaboard cities and towns of the state, originated with Hon. John A. Poor of Portland. His attention was drawn to the subject, early in 1861, and when the official note of Oct. 14, 1861, addressed by Mr. Seward, secretary of state, to the governors of the loyal states on the sea-coasts and lakes, was issued, Mr. Poor laid certain papers before Gov. Washburn, who promptly responded, and sent Hannibal Hamlin, Reuel Williams and Mr. Poor to Washington, as commissioners. They brought the matter properly before the secretary of war, and secured the appropriation. The fort was called Fort Popham, in honor of Gov. Popham, who, in 1608, erected a fort on the same site. Mr. Poor was further employed by Gov. Washburn as commissioner in 1862, and his report of Dec. 12, of that year, was laid before the legislature early in 1863 and printed. At the close of this session, he secured the adoption of vigorous resolutions, addressed to the authorities at Washington, which at once led to the supplying of proper guns and needed armament for the coast defences of the state,—a measure which had been neglected by the ordnance bureau of the United States year after year.

As most of the active militia of the state had been absorbed into the Federal service, it was found necessary to form several companies of home guards for coast defence. Fort McClary, at Kittery, was garrisoned on April 30, 1861; Fort Scammel, in Portland Harbor, on July 22, and Fort Sullivan, at Eastport, on Dec. 4. These companies were organized under the authority of the act passed at the extra session of the legislature, previously mentioned, and were recognized by the national government. Informal organizations of similar corps at Wiscasset and Boothbay were also recognized. Capt. R. H. Tucker, Jr., had command at the former place. Near the close of the year 1862, a patrol guard was detailed from Co. I, Capt. B. M. Flint, of Calais, for that city, to ward off a threatened lawless incursion across the eastern border of the state.

An event of much interest to the people of the state, and to the nation at large as well, occurred at the beginning of the year 1862, when Mr. Seward, secretary of state, granted permission for British troops to pass across the territory of Maine into Canada. As the movement of British troops to Canada at this time was in connection with the British demand for the release of Mason and Slidell, who had been taken from the British steamer Trent, the State of Maine was considerably agitated, and carefully inquired into the matter. The government explained that the principle on which this concession was made to Great Britain was that, when humanity or even convenience, renders it desirable for one nation to have a passage for its troops and munitions through another, it is a customary act of comity to grant it, if it can be done consistently with its own safety and welfare. There was no thought that the State of Maine would feel aggrieved; but if so, the directions would be modified.

During the progress of the war the Confederates made increasing efforts to acquire a navy, and already several powerful vessels flying their flag were inflicting much damage upon northern commerce. In the spring of 1863 rebel privateers appeared off the coast of Maine and attacked a number of vessels. On June 26, 1863, the crew of the Confederate bark Tacony, under the command of Lieut. Reade, entered Portland Harbor in the disguise of fishermen, on board a fishing schooner they had recently captured. After the capture of the schooner, their commander had transferred to her his crew and effects, and then burned the Tacony. The night after their unsuspected arrival in the harbor, they succeeded in capturing the United States revenue cutter, Caleb Cushing, an armed vessel, as she lay at anchor. Inquiry the next morning soon disclosed the method of her disappearance, and a volunteer fleet was sent in pursuit. Being a sailing vessel, the cutter was soon overhauled in the outer harbor. After a brief resistance, the Confederates set the cutter on fire and took to their boats in an attempt to reach the fishing schooner. The magazine of the cutter was stored with 400 pounds of powder, which exploded at 2 p. m. with terrific force, in full view of thousands of citizens who were watching the proceedings from vantage points on the shore. The daring Confederates, 23 in number, were captured before they could reach the schooner, and proved to be from the man-of-war, Florida. Their leader held a regular commission from the Confederate government and they could not, therefore, be adjudged pirates. After a short confinement at Fort Preble, they were exchanged. This episode increased the demand for a further strengthening of the state's seaboard defences by the national government, which was induced to act before the end of the year 1863, and Gov. Samuel Cony thus alluded to the work in his inaugural message: "Upon the call of this state by the resolves of the legislature touching the defenceless condition of her coast and northeastern frontier, and the urgent solicitation of my predecessor, the United States in addition to large expenditures upon the permanent fortifications in the harbor of Portland, at the mouth of the Kennebec river, and the narrows of the Penobscot, has constructed earthworks at Rockland, Belfast and Eastport, at each of which places two batteries of 5 guns each have been mounted, while both at Castine and Machiasport a single battery of 5 guns have been supplied."

A succession of victories by the Union armies in the latter part of 1861 and the earlier months of the following year, in both the east and west, led the North to believe that the Confederacy would soon collapse, and inspired the following resolution on the part of the Maine legislature, Feb. 18, 1862: "Resolved, That the legislature, for ourselves and in behalf of the state, tender to the gallant officers and soldiers of the army, and to the officers and soldiers of the navy of the United States, our warmest thanks for the brilliant victories recently won by their valor and skill in the States of Georgia, South Carolina, Missouri, North Carolina, Virginia, Kentucky and Tennessee, and that the governor be requested to order a salute to be fired in testimony of our appreciation of the honor and glory which these signal successes reflect on the arms of the Union."

In compliance with this resolve, a salute of 100 guns was fired at the capital. On April 3, 1862, the adjutant-general of the United States ordered the volunteer recruiting service in Maine to cease and all enlistments were suspended until May 21. Brig.-Gen. Milroy having been defeated on May 8, at the battle of Bull Pasture mountain, W. Va., by the forces under "Stonewall" Jackson, authority was given on the aforesaid date to raise the 16th regiment of infantry for three years service. No further call for troops was intimated.

One of the kaleidoscopic changes incident to the war now ensued. The army under Gen. Banks was routed at Winchester, May 25; Jackson's army escaped from Gens. Fremont and Shields and the genius of the wonderful Southern commander even inflicted a severe defeat on Gen. Shields; a few weeks later came the Seven Days' retreat of Gen. McClellan's army from the Chickahominy to the James, involving a series of terrible battles before Richmond. These events made it apparent that the war was far from ending, and that additional armies must be raised. July 2, 1862, the president issued a call for 300,000 men for three years, the quota assigned to Maine being 9,609. Within a few weeks a requisition was made upon Maine for her quota under this call, and the 16th regiment then ready, together with the 17th, 18th, 19th and 20th, authorized by General Orders, and numerous recruits for regiments in the field, furnished by cities, towns and plantations upon requirements based upon population, were accepted in satisfaction of the requisition. Meanwhile, an inspiring appeal to the people of the state had been issued on July 4, 1862, by Gov. Washburn, in which he said: "An additional number of troops is required by the exigency of the public service, and if raised immediately, it is believed by those who have the best means of knowledge, that the war will be brought to a speedy and glorious issue. * * * That her natural interests may be protected and advanced; that tranquility and peace may be restored throughout the land; that the Constitution and the Union, which have been to us all the source of unmeasured blessings, may be preserved; that Liberty, of which they were the inspiration and are the selected guardians, may be saved; and that the light of one great example may shine Brighter and brighter, to guide, cheer and to bless the nations; to aid in all these, I invoke the people of this state, a prompt and hearty response to this new demand upon their patriotism. And may they all unite in the work that is before them, each laboring in his own sphere, doing what he can by his example, influence and sympathy— proffering his treasure, his time, his strength, his heart and his highest hopes to the cause of his country.

General orders will be issued immediately, giving authority for raising new regiments of infantry and calling into actual service a portion of the ununiformed militia of the state."

Volunteering in all parts of the state was so prompt that the last of the above regiments, the 20th, was mustered into the service of the United States before the end of August. Before their organization was completed, the president, on Aug. 4, called for 300,000 militia, to be raised by draft, and to serve for nine months, unless sooner discharged. The quota of Maine, under this call, was 9,609, from which some deduction was made on account of the large number of enrolled militia in the merchant marine and the navy. Permission was also given to satisfy the requisition with volunteers, either in whole or in part. On Aug. 9 general orders were issued by the war department, which prescribed regulations for the enforcement of the draft, directed the selection of rendezvous for the troops, commandants for the encampments, and the enrolment of all able-bodied male citizens between the ages of eighteen and forty-five; it also directed, provisionally, the appointment of a commissioner from each county to superintend the drafting and hear and determine the excuses of persons claiming exemption from military duty. Under a law enacted by the legislature at its last session, all citizens subject to military duty had been enrolled in June, and only a supplementary enrolment was now found necessary to fulfil the requirements, hence no commissioners were appointed at this time in Maine. The enforcement of the draft was finally ordered for Sept. 10, but it was only found necessary to commence proceedings in a few towns, which were then deficient in their quotas. Under this stimulus, the municipal authorities of these towns, made arrangements to supply their quotas by voluntary enlistment, and without resort to the draft.

Three places of rendezvous were deemed sufficient:—"Camp Abraham Lincoln," at Portland, Col. John Lynch, commandant; "Camp E. D. Keyes," Augusta, Col. George W. Ricker, commandant; "Camp John Pope," Bangor, Col. Gideon Mayo, commandant. At Portland and Augusta, three regiments of nine months' troops were rendezvoused and organized at each encampment, and at Bangor, two regiments. As some of the towns were still deficient in their quotas at the close of October, a general order was issued, appointing a commissioner for each county to make a draft on Nov. 29, if any town should then be found wanting. These commissioners devoted their energies to such good purpose in facilitating enlistments for delinquent towns, that they found it unnecessary, in any instance, to resort to the harsh measures of the draft.

Seventy-seven cities and towns in the state even exceeded their quotas under the calls of July 2 and Aug. 4, sending from one to twenty-five men in excess of the demand, thus relieving other parts of the state. The town of Portage Lake had only one able-bodied man left in it; the town of Saco exceeded her quota under each call by no less than twenty-five men; and the town of Machias not only furnished its full quota with splendid promptness, but declared a willingness to respond to any future calls in like manner. Many towns had more men in the service than were required of them, but these recruits were credited to and received the bounty of other places, their places of residence never receiving the credit they deserved.

The citizens of Maine were divided into three parties at the election which took place on the second Monday of Sept., 1862: viz, the Republican, the Democratic, and the "War Democrats." The Republicans placed in nomination Abner Coburn as their candidate for governor; the "War Democrats" nominated Col. Charles D. Jameson, colonel of the 2nd Maine regiment; and the regular Democratic party nominated Bion Bradbury, who had previously failed to receive the nomination of the "War Democrats." The convention of the Republican party adopted a series of resolutions, in substance as follows: 1st.—inviting the patriotic citizens of Maine to unite on a simple basis to support the policy and principles characterizing the administration of Abraham Lincoln; 2nd.—that the rebellion must be put down at any cost; 3d.—expressing sympathy with, and praise of the American army and navy, and approving national and state

16

measures for their relief and reward; 4th.—expressing respect for and confidence in the present governor, Mr. Washburn; 5th.—expressing confidence in Hon. Abner Coburn, the nominee for governor. The resolutions adopted by the "War Democrats," expressed "unwavering support to the government in all necessary and proper efforts to subdue the existing rebellion and vindicate the authority of the Constitution and Union over every inch of territory in the United States, and gratitude to our army and navy," but voiced resistance to "all measures and efforts to convert this war for the Union into a crusade for negro emancipation;" approved the "patriotic course of the brave Gen. McClellan," and "viewed with detestation and scorn the wicked attempts of scheming politicians to undermine and weaken him and his army in their brave efforts for the vindication of the Union." The resolutions of the regular Democrats declared among other things, "That the purpose of the Democratic party is the restoration of the Union as it was, and the preservation of the Constitution as it is; and to secure these objects we will stand shoulder to shoulder with Union men everywhere in support of the Federal government in maintaining its safety, integrity, and legitimate authority by all constitutional means." The platform recited certain of the Bill of Rights of the Federal constitution, and "condemned and denounced the repeated and gross violation by the executive of the United States, of the said rights thus secured by the constitution; and also repudiated the monstrous dogma that in time of war the constitution is suspended, or its powers in any respect enlarged beyond the letter and true meaning of that instrument;" etc. At the election held on Sept. 8, Coburn received 45,534 votes; Jameson, 7,178, and Bradbury, 32,331, a Republican majority over both the others of 6,025. Four Republican Congressmen, one Democratic Congressman, and a Republican majority of 81 in the state legislature were elected at the same time.

By the close of the year 1862, there had been sent into the field from the State of Maine, twenty-seven regiments of infantry, one regiment of cavalry, one regiment of heavy artillery, six batteries, and one company of sharpshooters, exceeding 30,000 men. These were all volunteer troops, and were distributed in Virginia on the Peninsula; southwest of Washington; at Port Royal, S. C.; Fernandina and Pensacola, Fla., and at New Orleans. In addition to the troops above mentioned, a considerable number were also recruited for regiments in the field, which had become depleted from active service.

The draft was enforced by the general government under the conscription law for the first time in the year 1863. In June of this year, Lee's great army of nearly 100,000 men had crossed the Potomac and his advanced corps under Ewell had entered Pennsylvania. The authorities at Washington were much alarmed by the presence of this army on their north and on June 29 a draft of 100,000 men was ordered by the war department. The draft proceeded in Maine, during the summer months, in a generally peaceable and orderly manner. Maj. J. W. T. Gardiner was appointed acting assistant provost-marshal-general of Maine, and boards of enrolment were organized by the United States in the five congressional districts of the state. The only resistance made to the enforcement of the draft was in the towns of Kingfield, Freeman and Salem, in the 2nd district, when, in July, the malcontents to the number of a few score of men rallied at Kingston and made some show of armed rebellion. This uprising was promptly subdued by a force of men made up of Co. G, 3d division of the state militia (composed chiefly of returned veterans), and a detail of United States regulars; the whole under the command of Post Adjt. Webber, on the staff of Maj. Gardiner. The number of men held for service or accepted as substitutes under the draft, was about 2,500. As many towns had voted in public meeting to pay the commutations of such of their citizens as might be drafted, Gov. Coburn, in view of the trouble which might result from this action, propounded the two following questions to the justices of the Supreme Court: 1.—"Has a city or town any legal right to pledge its credit to raise money for the purpose of paying the commutations of such of its citizens as may be drafted into the service of the United States under the law aforesaid? 2.—Has a city or town any legal right to raise money by taxation to provide commutations for such of its citizens as may be drafted?"

The court ruled that Congress had full power, under the constitution, "to command all the resources of the nation, the lives of its citizens, to prevent, by any and all proper means, that fearful anarchy which would be so imminent if its dissolution should become an accomplished fact;" that the liability to serve, procure a substitute, or pay the commutation fee, as created by the Enrolment act of March 3 was of a purely personal nature; that this was "an act to raise soldiers, not to raise money," etc. Each of the questions was answered in the negative.

Following the draft, another call for troops was made by the president on Oct. 17, for 300,000 volunteers to serve for three years. This gave rise to an eloquent proclamation from Gov. Coburn which opened as follows: "Of this additional force Maine is expected to furnish her quota, and she will not disappoint that expectation. Now, as heretofore, her patriotic men will respond to the call, and promptly furnish her full share of the force necessary to vindicate the integrity of our government, and maintain the supremacy of the laws of the Union.

"Our people, with almost entire unanimity, have determined that the present rebellion shall be suppressed, and that the Union which it was designed to destroy, shall be maintained. For this purpose they entered upon the contest, and to this end they will persevere until the object be accomplished, and until the world shall be satisfied that free men can endure more, and persevere longer for the preservation of free government, than can the most determined and desperate traitor for its destruction.

"The length of the conflict is not to be measured by years, but by events. Treason is to be put down, and to that end should all the measures of the government be subservient."

Pending the draft in 1863, Gov. Coburn received permission through a general order of the war department, to recruit the 29th and 30th regiments of infantry, 2nd regiment of cavalry, and 7th battery of light artillery, which organizations were termed veteran volunteers, and furnished with "service chevrons" by the war department, to be worn as a badge of honorable distinction, as was done with all men who reenlisted. By the end of the year the above troops were nearly ready for the field and in addition a large number of men were enlisted for regiments already at the front. Ten Maine regiments were mustered out of the service of the United States during the year 1863, the terms of their enlistments having expired, and at the close of the year, there remained in active service sixteen regiments and one battalion of infantry, one regiment and one company of cavalry, one regiment of heavy and six batteries of light artillery, and one company of sharpshooters. In addition to the government bounty of $402 for veteran recruits and $302 for new recruits, Maine offered in October, 1863, a bounty of $100 to all recruits entering incomplete organizations then in the state, and $55 to recruits entering regiments or corps in the field; besides this, as in 1862, numerous cities and towns paid extra bounties to recruits enlisted within their limits, anticipating legislative grants for legal authority in such cases. It had been hoped in this manner to escape any resort to the draft in Maine. As in previous years, many of the seafaring population entered the naval service.

When the war broke out, the bonded state debt was in round numbers about $700,000. This was increased by expenses incidental to the war to $1,472,000 on Jan. 1, 1863, and during that year there was added a further war debt of $950,000, making the total debt of the state, on Jan. 1, 1864, $2,422,000. The legislature of 1863 increased the state tax of that year over the tax of the previous year by the addition of a mill on the dollar of valuation. It also renewed the act of the previous year, exempting for another year the state banks from the severe penalties imposed by their charters in the event of their suspending specie payments. This legislature also remitted one-half of the state tax imposed upon the banks by their charters, as Congress had imposed a tax upon the circulation and deposits of the local banks.

The Republican state convention of 1863 voted unanimously to sustain the national administration in its efforts to subdue the rebellion, and placed in nomination for governor Samuel Cony, who had in the previous year been a prominent member of the party known as "War Democrats," and had made an active canvass of the state in favor of Col. Jameson. The Republicans and the War Democrats united in the canvass this year under the name of the Union party. The Democrats renominated their candidate of the previous year, Bion Bradbury, and adopted resolutions announcing their devotion to the Constitution and the Union, but severely denouncing many of the war measures of the Government. They declared that in the opinion of the convention the war was conducted by the present administration "not for the restoration of the Union, but for the abolition of slavery and the destruction of the Union." In the election which followed on Sept. 14, Cony received 67,916 votes, and Bradbury 50,366—a majority for Cony of 17,550. The Union party also had a majority of 118 on joint ballot in the legislature, elected at the same time.

Among the more important war measures passed by the legislature of 1864 was an act authorizing Maine soldiers in the field to vote for electors of president and vice-president; also a resolve by a two-thirds vote providing for an amendment to the constitution of the state, so as to allow soldiers absent from the state, except those in the regular army of the United States, to vote for governor and other state and county officers. This amendment was ratified by the people by a majority of 45,303. The whole number of votes cast by soldiers was reported to be 4,915. A law was also enacted for the payment by the state of a uniform bounty of $300 to any person enlisting under any calls except those made prior to Feb. 1, 1864. This was done to correct the practice which had arisen in large cities and towns, which in their anxiety to avoid the draft outbid each other in the amount of bounties, thus depriving the poorer towns of the ability to fill their quotas. The law operated well until the call of July 18, 1864, under which recruits were taken for one year. The state offered only $100 for this class of recruits, which proved to be insufficient, and the old methods were again resorted to by the cities and towns.

Under Gov. Cony's administration in 1864 six companies of cavalry were raised late in the winter for Baker's D. C. cavalry, in addition to one raised by his predecessor. The 31st and 32nd regiments of infantry were also raised under the call of Feb. 1, 1864. Ewell's daring raid up the Shenandoah Valley early in July, 1864, during which he invaded Maryland and the District of Columbia and severed the communications of Washington with the North, so alarmed Gov. Cony that he issued a proclamation declaring the national capital in danger, and calling for volunteers for 100 days' service for its protection. A general response was made throughout the state; but fortunately the danger proved of short duration, as the invading force was small and retired in a few days into Virginia, with a mass of plunder, without forcing Grant to release his hold upon Petersburg. On July 18, the president issued his call for 500,000 men to serve one, two and three years, and all further action upon the governor's proclamation was at once suspended.

During the year 1864, Maine contributed to the military and naval service of the country an aggregate of 18,904 men, of whom 3,380 were enlisted under the call of Oct., 1863, and 3,525 were veteran soldiers, who reenlisted. Enlistments for the navy numbered 1,846. Allowances of credits for naval enlistments anterior to 1864 were made to the number of 3,675. The term of their original enlistment having expired, the 3d, 4th, 5th, 6th, 7th, 12th,

13th and 14th infantry regiments were mustered out of the service during the year. A large portion of these organizations had reenlisted, and these, together with others whose terms of enlistment had not yet expired, were transferred to other regiments, so that only about 2,000 men all told were thus lost to the army. By the close of this year the state had furnished for the military and naval service more than 61,000 men, a number nearly equal to one-tenth of her whole population, and an excess of several hundred over all calls. By a resolve approved March 19, 1864, the treasurer of the state was authorized to borrow $3,000,000 by the issue of six per cent, bonds payable in 25 years. He sold bonds to the amount of $2,765,000, which increased the funded debt of the state to $5,137,000 on Jan. 1, 1865. At the same date the total ascertained funded and floating debt amounted to $5,714,625.31.

Toward the close of the year 1864, so much of the territory of the Confederacy had fallen into Union hands, that a large number of troops were required to occupy and garrison it effectively. Moreover, it was believed that the rebellion could be finally crushed with larger armies, and so President Lincoln called for 300,000 more men on Dec. 19. Maine did her share in meeting this demand, but, like most of the other states, did not complete her full quota, as the necessity for more men had ceased to exist.

The Republican state convention assembled at Portland on June 29, and renominated Samuel Cony for governor by acclamation. The Democrats, in their convention at Bangor on Aug. 16, unanimously nominated for governor, Joseph Howard of Portland. After a political campaign conducted with unusual earnestness until the presidential election in November, Gov. Cony was reelected on Sept. 12, by a majority of 15,913, and the legislature chosen at the same time showed a Republican majority of 118 on joint ballot. The vote for presidential electors in November gave a Republican majority of 17,592, and the electors chosen cast the vote of the state for Abraham Lincoln for president, and Andrew Johnson for vice-president. William P. Fessenden, having resigned as U. S. Senator from Maine to accept the office of secretary of the treasury, Gov. Cony appointed Nathan A. Farwell in his place.

An attempt was made to rob the bank at Calais, on July 18, by a small party of Confederate raiders from St. John, N. B., led by one Collins, a captain in a Mississippi regiment. The daring plan was frustrated, but led to an uneasy feeling along the north-eastern and eastern frontier. Volunteer organizations were formed in Eastport, Calais, Belfast, and other border towns to patrol the streets at night, and the regular police force was increased and armed. In view of the possible danger from this source, Gov. Cony ordered several companies of home guards to stand ready to move to any part of the state at a moment's warning.

This brief narrative of the splendid part Maine took in the War of the Rebellion must now be brought to a close. Elsewhere in this work will be given in detail the splendid services of some of her noble sons, among them the gallant Gen. O. O. Howard, conspicuous at Gettysburg, and afterwards in the campaigns of the Southwest, where he rose to the command of one of the armies under Sherman; Gen. Hiram G. Berry, whose military talents and substantial service brought him to high command, and whose death on the field of Chancellorsville was a sore loss to the army; Gen. Joshua L. Chamberlain, whose military experience and honors won were altogether remarkable; and many others equally worthy of mention here did the limits of this sketch permit. It may be remarked that three sons of Senator Fessenden and two of Senator Hamlin served with distinction, one of each family giving his life for the cause.

Soon after the capitulation of General Lee, the Maine troops began to return home to their families and friends. The regiments returned, sunburned, ragged and worn, sacred for their losses and crowned with honor. Many flags had been captured, but not one had been lost, by the gallant sons of Maine.

The troops furnished by Maine to the Union army during the progress of the war comprised two regiments of cavalry; one regiment of heavy artillery; three companies of garrison artillery; one battalion of seven batteries of light artillery; one battalion of six companies of sharpshooters; thirty regiments and sixteen companies of infantry, inclusive of the coastguard battalion of seven companies, a total of 72,114; or, reduced to a three years standard, 56,776. In addition to the above, the state was credited with a total of 6,750 men in the navy and marine corps, and also furnished about 800 men for the 1st D. C. cavalry, an independent organization under the command of Col. L. C. Baker. It will thus be seen that Maine contributed considerably more than one-tenth of her total population to the service of the nation. Of the numbers above given, 2,801 were killed or died of wounds, according to the army list; 4,521 died of disease; and 6,642 were mustered out for disabilities resulting from casualties occurring in service or from sickness.

The financial credit of the state was well sustained throughout the war, notwithstanding upwards of $15,000,000 were contributed in one way or another by her inhabitants to the national cause. The funded debt of the state on Jan. 1, 1861, was $699,500, as against $5,164,500 on Jan. 1, 1866, the increase of $4,465,000 being due altogether to the extraordinary expenses growing out of the war. From Jan. 1, 1861, to Jan. 1, 1866, the state expended for war purposes a total of $7,357,-572, of which $4,578,636 were paid for bounties. The amount advanced by cities and towns for aid to families of soldiers to Jan. 1, 1865, was $1,599,536. In addition to the above, the cities and towns of the state contracted a debt of not less than $6,556,183 for bounties. No one would have deemed it possible that the state of Maine could have sent so many troops into the field, or that she could raise such vast sums of money to meet the expenses of the war.

Soon after the outbreak of the war, arrangements were made to transmit such portions of the pay of persons in service as they chose to allot for the benefit of their families or themselves. State and municipal authorities cordially cooperated with the war department in securing the acquiescence of soldiers in this wise arrangement for the welfare of themselves and families.

Everything possible was done by the state authorities and by the better portion of the citizens of both sexes in aid of the sick and wounded soldiers, and to improve the sanitary conditions of Maine troops in the field. State agencies for the relief of the disabled and destitute soldiers of the state were maintained at New York, Philadelphia and Washington. Among the many who labored in this splendid work, were George R. Davis, agent of the U. S. Sanitary Commission, Portland; Cols. Frank E. Howe of the New England Soldier's Relief Association, New York; Robert R. Corson, Philadelphia; and Charles F. Mudge of the special relief department of the U. S. Sanitary Commission, Boston. The Washington Relief Association, composed of citizens of Maine residing in Washington, was a potent agency for good in relieving the wants of wounded, sick and destitute soldiers in and near that city.

In conclusion, it may be truly said that Maine gave unstintedly of her treasure of her best blood to secure the perpetuation of the Union. Nearly every home had its martyr, a willing sacrifice on the altar of country. The record of the Pine Tree State throughout the long four-years' struggle was indeed a glorious one, and will challenge comparison with that of any other of the loyal states.

RECORD OF MAINE
REGIMENTS

FIRST INFANTRY

Col., Nathaniel J. Jackson; Lieut.-Col., Albion Witham; Maj., George G. Bailey. This regiment was organized for active service on April 28, 1861, and was mustered into the United States service for three months, May 3, at Portland. Its departure from the state was somewhat delayed by sickness and it did not leave for the seat of war until June 1. It was raised at a time when Washington was in great danger, when a feeling of gloom pervaded the North, and every man who enlisted fully expected that the regiment would be called into active service at the front. It numbered 779 men. Eight of its companies were highly esteemed organizations in the state militia before entering the service of the United States. Two were of recent organization and enlisted to make up the quota of the regiment. Their camp was at Westbrook, near the marine hospital, and was called Camp Washburn, in honor of the governor. On their way to Washington, they were the recipients of marked attention at Newburyport, the birthplace of Col. Jackson, at New York, Philadelphia, and in fact all along the route. Both at Newburyport and New York they were presented with beautiful American flags. At Baltimore they marched over the same route as the 6th Mass., but were not molested. Soon after their arrival in Washington, they went into camp on Meridian Hill. Though eager and ready, the regiment was not allowed to participate in the first battle of Bull Run, as it was not thought best to withdraw it from the defenses of Washington. The 1st Me. was noted for its fine discipline and was regarded as a model regiment. After Bull Run it was stationed for a time to guard the Long Bridge, which was considered the post of honor. It performed necessary guard duty at exposed points in the immediate vicinity of the capital until Aug. 1, when the term of enlistment having expired it returned to Portland, and was mustered out on the 5th. The men returned bronzed and healthy, not a single one missing. Though enlisted in the state service for two years, they could not be moved outside the state after the expiration of their three months' muster in, and they were disbanded. On the formation of new regiments, a large proportion of the officers and men reenlisted in other organizations. Col. Jackson was soon after placed in command of the 5th infantry and had a long and honorable record. He was subsequently promoted to brigadier-general, and later placed in command of the rendezvous camp at Ricker's island, New York harbor.

SECOND INFANTRY

Col., Charles D. Jameson; Lieut.-Col., Charles W. Roberts; Maj., George Varney. Numerically the second, this was in fact the first regiment to leave the state for the front. It was raised within the limits of the first militia division of the state and was rendezvoused at Bangor. Companies A, B, C, D and I belonged to Col. Jameson's old command, and were reorganized for service in this regiment. The others were new companies. It completed its organization and left the state May 14, 1861. Like the 1st, it originally enlisted for three months, but on May 28, was mustered into the United States service for two years. The 2nd, during its two years' term of service, saw much hard service and participated in eleven bloody and hard-fought battles, besides numerous skirmishes and scouting expeditions. It never received a word of censure and invariably distinguished itself. A list of the important battles in which it was engaged includes the first and second Bull Run, Hall's Hill, Yorktown, Hanover Court House, Gaines' Mill, Malvern Hill, Antietam, Fredericksburg and Chancellorsville. The magnificent fighting record of the 2nd was largely due to the efficiency of its officers. It showed the stuff it was made of in its first battle at Bull Run. Col. Keyes, who commanded the brigade which included the 2nd Me., says in his official report of the battle: "The gallantry with which the 2nd regiment of Maine volunteers charged up the hill upon the enemy's artillery and infantry, was never in my opinion surpassed." Col. Jameson, the first volunteer and the first colonel in the field from Maine, was commissioned brigadier-general of volunteers for gallantry displayed in this, his first battle. Lieut.-Col. Roberts succeeded to the command of the regiment, and after his resignation and honorable discharge, Jan. 10, 1863, Lieut.-Col. Varney was promoted to the colonelcy of the regiment, and Maj. Sargent was commissioned lieutenant-colonel, the majorship being left vacant on account of the reduced condition of the regiment. On July 18, 1862, Capt. Chaplin, who had succeeded Varney in that command, was discharged to enable him to accept the command of the 18th Me., then being raised, and Capt. Sargent of Co. G was promoted to fill the vacancy. Some of the men became discontented three months after leaving the state from seeing three months' men from other states returning home. Sixty-six claimed their time had expired, became insubordinate, and were sentenced to Tortugas; but this sentence was later commuted to a transfer to the 2nd N. Y., where they served about a year and then returned and served faithfully with the regiment for the remainder of the term. Co. I became greatly reduced in numbers in Oct., 1861, and the officers having resigned, it was disbanded. Capt. Daniel White of Bangor raised a new company which took its place in December of that year. On July 28, 1862, the effective strength of the 2nd became reduced to 257 rifles and came out of the battle of Second Bull Run with but 137 men able to carry arms. This is most convincing evidence of the trying service to which they were subjected. The regiment was mustered out June 4, and 9, 1863. In all 1,228 men were mustered in, of whom 275 returned and were mustered out; 120 were mustered in for three years and transferred to the 20th Me.

THIRD INFANTRY

Col., Oliver O. Howard; Lieut.-Col., Isaac N. Tucker; Maj., Henry G. Staples. This regiment responded to the first call for troops with promptness and alacrity. It was rendezvoused on the state house grounds at Augusta and was composed mainly of Kennebec lumbermen. The regiment was most fortunate in having for its colonel Oliver O. Howard, who rose rapidly to the rank of major-general and gained for himself a name distinguished among the nation's heroes. During the long three years' service the regiment was successively commanded by Maj. Staples and Capt. Moses B. Lakeman of Co. I, Lieut.-Col. Tucker having resigned to become brigade quartermaster. On the resignation of Lieut.-Col. Tucker, Capt. Sampson of Co. D, Capt. Lakeman and Adjt. Burt served as lieutenant-colonel in the order named. Succeeding Henry G. Staples as major were Adjt. Burt and Capt. William C. Morgan. Of the original companies of the regiment Co. A (Bath City Greys) had existed under former militia laws and the others were new organizations. The regiment was mustered into the United States service on June 4, 1861, and left the state for the front the next day. Perhaps no regiment from the state saw more fighting or rendered more distinguished service. From the first battle of Bull Run, until the battle of Cold Harbor, June 3, 1864, the regiment participated in most of the important battles and movements of the Army of the Potomac. The operations of the so-called "Stove-Pipe Artillery" commenced with this regiment. While encamped at Flag Hill, Va., they employed the ruse of mounting a stove-pipe on wheels, and drew 12 shots from the enemy at their cannon. The loss of the 3d in killed and wounded at the battle of Fair Oaks was nearly one-third of the men engaged. It was in this engagement that Sergt.-Maj. F. W. Haskell of Waterville so greatly distinguished himself as to win the commendation of his colonel and of the entire regiment. The 3d gave an excellent account of itself in the battle of Gettysburg. At the close of the second day's fighting Gen. Sickles declared that, "The little 3d Me. saved the army today." Its loss at Gettysburg was 113 killed, wounded and missing. On the return of the regiment to Augusta, June 11, 1864, only 17 officers and 176 enlisted men were left to be mustered out. Sixty-four of these men reenlisted, and together with the recruits were transferred to the 17th Me. Not one of the original field and staff officers returned with the regiment and only one of the original captains—the veteran Moses B. Lakeman—who returned in command of the regiment.

FOURTH INFANTRY

Col. Hiram G. Berry; Lieut.-Col., Thomas H. Marshall; Maj., Frank S. Nickerson. This regiment was organized for active service May 8, 1861, and was mustered into the United States service on June 15 at Rockland. Co. A (Belfast Artillery), Co. K (Belfast City (Grays), and Co. F (Brooks Light Infantry), had formed part of the state militia, but the other companies were without previous experience. The regiment left Rockland for Washington on June 17, and was armed with the Springfield smooth-bore musket. Passing through New York, it was presented with two beautiful flags. It participated in all the important battles of the Army of the Potomac during its three years' term of service. Gen. Kearney wrote as follows of the conduct of its gallant colonel at Bull Run: "Col. Berry manifested such a genius for war, and such a pertinacity in the fight, as proved him fit for high command." It is stated that the 4th Me. saved the day at Williamsburg, while at Fair Oaks, White Oak Swamp, Gaines' Mill, Glendale, Gettysburg, the Wilderness, and on many other bloody fields it rendered magnificent service. The heroic commander of the regiment, Hiram G. Berry, was killed amid the awful carnage of the battle of Chancellorsville, having attained to the rank of major-general and being esteemed one of the most brilliant officers in the service. On June 25, 1864, the regiment arrived in Rockland, its term of service having expired on the 15th, and alter being furloughed were mustered out on July 19. It returned under we command of Elijah Walker, who had gone out as captain of Co B. There were 46 officers in the regiment, including 10 recruits; privates of the original organization, 966; recruits, 513; total, 1,525. Number of officers mustered out, 17; prisoners of war, 2; privates mustered out, 224; prisoners 37; officers discharged, 5; resigned, 41; privates discharged for disability,. 366; privates transferred to other commands, 435, officers died of wounds, 14; of disease, 2; privates died of wounds, 139; of disease, 112 privates deserted, 131. Total, 1,525. The number of officers lost by casualties during the service of the regiment was 65; mustered out July 19, 1864, 17; prisoners of war, 2. Total, 84. Thirty-eight officers were promoted from the ranks.

FIFTH INFANTRY

Cols., Mark H. Dunnell, Nathaniel J. Jackson, Edward A. Scammon, Clark S. Edwards; Lieut.-Cols., Edwin Illsley, William S. Heath, Edward A. Scammon, Clark S. Edwards, Capt. Millett of Co. A; Majs., Samuel C. Hamilton, Edward A. Scammon, Clark S. Edwards, Capt. Millett, A. S. Daggett. This regiment was recruited from the third militia division of the state. It was mustered into the service of the United States on June 24, 1861, and numbered 1,046 men. It was made up entirely of new companies and was raised at a time when a spirit of intense patriotism prevailed throughout the state, so that little exertion was required to fill its ranks. It left Maine for Washington on June 26, fully equipped and armed with Springfield muskets and bayonets. On its way through New York city it was the recipient of a beautiful flag, presented by the loyal sons of Maine there resident. It remained in camp at Meridian Hill, Washington, until July 5, when it commenced its march to the battlefield of Bull Run. During its three years of severe service, it was engaged in eleven pitched battles and eight skirmishes, prior to its participation in the terrible campaign of the Wilderness under Grant. Its list of battles includes First Bull Run, West Point, Gaines' Mill, Charles City Cross-Roads, Crampton's Gap, Antietam, Fredericksburg, Salem Heights, Gettysburg, Rappahannock Station, Wilderness, Spottsylvania Court House and Cold Harbor. In the battle of Gaines' Mill the 5th lost 10 killed, 69 wounded and 16 missing, its gallant Col. Jackson was carried wounded from the field and Lieut.-Col. Heath was among the killed. At Rappahannock Station, the regiment was conspicuous for its gallantry, and captured 4 standards of the enemy. The flags were presented to Gen. Meade, who said: "In the name of the army and the country I thank you for the services you have rendered, particularly for the example you have set and which I doubt not on future occasions will be followed and emulated." In a gallant charge on the enemy's works at Spottsylvania Court House, more than half of the regiment was lost in crossing an open field subject to a raking fire of canister, but it captured the works, and took 2 flags and a large number of prisoners. In addition to the 6 captured flags, the 5th had the record of taking more men prisoners than it carried on its own rolls. It left the front near Petersburg, June 22, 1864, and started for home, arriving in Portland on the 28th with 216 men, who were mustered out of service, July 27, 1864, the veterans and recruits having been transferred to the 7th Me. During its term of service it had received some 500 recruits.

SIXTH INFANTRY

Cols., Abner Knowles, Hiram Burnham, Benjamin F. Harris; Lieut.-Cols., Hiram Burnham, Charles H. Chandler, Benjamin F. Harris; Majs., George Fuller (commissioned, but never mustered in), Frank Pierce, Benjamin F. Harris, Joel A. Hancock, George Fuller, Theo. Lincoln, Jr. (commissioned, but never mustered in), Frank Pierce, Benjamin F. Harris, Joel A. Hancock, George Fuller, Theo. Lincoln, Jr. This regiment was composed principally of

34

the hardy lumbermen of the Penobscot valley and the eastern portion of the state, who were quick to respond to the first call to arms. Before its organization it was made up of two battalions of five companies each, rendezvousing respectively at the state arsenal, Bangor, and Fort Sullivan, Eastport. Under a general order from Adjt.-Gen. Hodsdon, June 28, 1861, both battalions were removed to Portland and organized into a regiment for active service. On July 12-15, 1861, it was mustered into the service of the United States and on the 17th left for Washington. En route through New York city, the regiment was presented with a handsome standard by the sons of Maine in that city. It arrived in Washington on the 19th and was stationed at Chain Bridge on the Potomac, where it remained until Sept. 3. Through the fall and winter of 1861-62 it occupied Fort Griffin, and in March, 1862, was put into Hancock's brigade, Smith's division, and joined in the advance on Manassas. A little later it was attached to the 4th corps under Gen. E. D. Keyes, and advanced with the rest of the army on Yorktown on April 4, 1862. For the remainder of its three years the regiment saw the most arduous and active service. It participated in ten general engagements and in a great many skirmishes. On April 5-7, 1862, it was engaged in skirmishing and reconnaissances at the siege of Yorktown, and subsequently took part in the engagements at Lee's mills, Williamsburg, Garnett's farm, White Oak bridge, Antietam and Fredericksburg. From Feb. 2 to May 11, 1863, it was with the "Light Division," and during this period took an honorable part in the battle of Chancellorsville, where it lost 128 officers and men killed and wounded. Other important battles in which the 6th was engaged were Rappahannock Station, where it lost 16 officers and 123 men; Wilderness, Spottsylvania Court House, where it lost a few men, and two days later in an attack on the enemy's works on the right, it lost 125 in killed, wounded and missing. On June 12, 1864, the regiment only numbered 70 men, and was under fire for eight hours, supporting Gen. Hancock's corps, losing 16 officers and men. The original members of the regiment were mustered out on Aug. 15, 1864, and the veterans and recruits to the number of 238 men, were transferred to the 7th Me. afterwards organized as the 1st regiment veteran volunteers.

Col., Edwin C. Mason; Lieut.-Cols., Thomas H. Marshall, Selden Connor, Thomas W. Hyde; Majs., Thomas W. Hyde, James P. Jones (known in the army as the "fighting Quaker"), Stephen C. Fletcher. This regiment was raised irrespective of divisional limits, and was organized at Augusta, Aug. 21, 1861, to serve three years. It left the state Aug. 23, 1861 and arrived in Baltimore on the 25th. It remained here until Oct. 25, when it was moved to Washington. Nov. 7th, it crossed the Potomac into Virginia and went into" camp near Lewinsville, Fairfax county, where it remained until March 10, 1862, engaged in picket duty, scouting and drilling. Sickness and death had been prevalent in its ranks, and Co. F became so reduced in numbers it was disbanded, a new company raised by Capt Fletcher of Skowhegan, being mustered into service Jan. 23, 1862, in Its place. March 23, 1862, the regiment embarked for Fortress Monroe, preparatory to the Peninsular campaign. It was at this time in the 3d brigade, 2nd division, 6th provisional corps, the division being under the command of Gen. Smith. On April 4, 1862, it joined in the advance on Richmond, and led the advance on the Yorktown line of defenses on April 5. The next day it was under the fire of Fort Lee on Warwick creek, and afterwards participated in the siege of Yorktown, holding a position near Dam No. 3, "the key of the line", until the enemy evacuated. For its gallantry at the battle of Williamsburg, the 7th received the personal thanks of Gen. McClellan. On May 24, it won more glory at the first battle at Mechanicsville and during June it was almost daily engaged with the enemy, who tried to shell it from its position on the left bank of the Chickahominy. On the withdrawal of the army from Richmond, the 7th participated in the battles of Savage Station, White Oak Swamp and Malvern Hill. In the autumn it joined in the Maryland campaign, took part in the battles of South Mountain and Antietam, losing at the latter battle, 11 officers and 100 enlisted men out of 15 officers and 166 enlisted men present. In Oct., 1862, it became so reduced in numbers it was sent to Portland, Me., to recruit, and on Jan. 21, 1863, it left Portland with a battalion of five companies filled by consolidation and rejoined its old command, 3d brigade, 2nd division, 6th corps, at White Oak Church, Va. May 2, 1863, it was in the storming party which carried the enemy's works on Cemetery and Marye's Heights

36

near Fredericksburg, and engaged the enemy on the 4th in a desperate struggle near Chancellorsville. On May 23, Co. F under Capt. Fletcher, having been reorganized at Portland, rejoined the battalion. It participated in the Pennsylvania campaign, taking part in the battles of Rappahannock Station, Locust Grove, Mine Run and numerous skirmishes. The following year it was with Grant in the relentless advance on Richmond, and was engaged in the battles of the Wilderness, Spottsylvania Court House, Cold Harbor, and the attacks on the Weldon railroad. July 11, 1864, the regiment returned to Washington, and assisted in the defeat of the enemy on its nearest approach to the capital. On the 13th, it marched up the Potomac, through Snicker's gap to the Shenandoah, and was back in Washington on the 23d. On the 26th, it again started up the Potomac, crossed at Harper's Ferry on the 29th, and marched to the vicinity of Charlestown, where it remained until its original term of service expired on Aug. 21, 1864, when it returned to Maine and was mustered out of service Sept. 5, at Augusta. The reenlisted men and recruits of the regiment were consolidated with battalions of the 5th and 6th regiments to form the 1st veteran infantry in Sept., 1864.

EIGHTH INFANTRY

Cols., Lee Strickland, John D. Rust, Henry Boynton, William M. McArthur; Lieut.-Cols., John D. Rust, Ephraim W. Woodman, Joseph F. Twitchell, John Hemingway, Henry Boynton, William M. McArthur, Edward A. True; Majs., Joseph S. Rice, Ephraim W. Woodman, Joseph F. Twitchell, John Hemingway, Henry Boynton, William M. McArthur, Edward A. True. This regiment was made up of companies from different parts of the state, and was organized at Augusta, Sept. 7, 1861, to serve three years. It entered the service with 770 enlisted men, and in bravery and efficiency was excelled by few, if any regiments in the service. It left the state Sept. 10, for Hempstead, Long Island, N. Y., and subsequently for Fortress Monroe, Va., where it formed a part of Gen. T. W. Sherman's expedition to Port Royal, S. C., which sailed on Oct. 29, and landed at Hilton Head Nov. 8, 1861. For several months the men were engaged in throwing up breastworks and building fortifications. On May 1, 1862, they moved to Tybee Island in the Savannah river, and took a prominent part in the attack on and capture of Fort Pulaski, one of the defenses of Savannah. From this time until the spring of 1864, the regiment was employed for the most part in doing guard duty at Hilton Head and Beaufort, S. C. and at Jacksonville, Fla. It suffered much sickness as the result of the exposures of the spring campaign in 1862, and from diseases contracted in a southern climate. In Nov., 1862, about 300 well drilled and disciplined recruits were sent to the regiment from Maine. In Nov., 1863, while at Beaufort, S. C, its ranks were again replenished by the addition of nearly 200 drafted men, who proved excellent soldiers. In March, 1864, 16 officers and 330 enlisted men, who had reenlisted for a term of three years, received a furlough of 35 days and returned to their homes. In April, 1864, the 8th was transferred to the Department of Virginia, and on May 4, moved to Bermuda Hundred, where it took part in all the active operations of the Army of the James. Sixty veterans, whose term of service had expired, returned to the state, and were mustered out of service on Sept. 15, 1864. The regiment was still large enough, however, to retain its organization as many men had reenlisted and it had received 570 recruits. Until the surrender of Lee at Appomattox, it was engaged in numerous skirmishes and arduous picket and guard duties, and took part in the following important engagements: Drewry's Bluff, losing 96 men, killed, wounded and prisoners; Cold Harbor, where it lost 79 men; the operations before Petersburg, losing 50 men; Chaffin's Farm; Fair Oaks, where it again lost heavily, Spring Hill; capture of Forts Gregg and Baldwin, Rice's Station and Appomattox Court House. After Lee's surrender, it was at Richmond until Aug., 1865, at Manchester until the following November, and at Fortress Monroe until Jan. 18, 1866, when the men were mustered out and proceeded to Augusta, Me., where they were paid and finally discharged.

NINTH INFANTRY

Cols., Rishworth Rice, Jan. 2, 1863, Horatio Bisbee, Jr., Sabine Emery, George F. Granger; Lieut.-Cols., Coleman Hardigg, Horatio Bisbee, Jr., Sabine Emery, Zina H. Robinson, George F. Granger, Joseph Noble; Majs., Sabine Emery, Zina H. Robinson, Geo. F. Granger, Joseph Noble, Geo. B. Dyer. This regiment was raised at large and was organized at Augusta, Sept. 22, 1861, to serve three years.. In less than two weeks from the arrival of the first company at Augusta, the 9th was on its way to Washington, with more than 1,000 men in its ranks. The original members (except veterans) numbering 158 men were mustered out of service Sept. 27, 1864, and the regiment composed of veterans and recruits, retained in service until July 13, 1865, when it was mustered out under orders from the war department. The 3d company of unassigned infantry, organized Sept. 30, 1864, was assigned to this regiment as Co. K, and was mustered out June 30, 1865. Soon after its arrival in Washington (Sept. 26), the regiment was assigned to Gen. T. W. Sherman's expedition for the capture of Port Royal, S. C., and landed at Hilton Head, S. C., Nov. 8, 1861. On Feb. 7, 1862, it went to Warsaw island, off the coast of Georgia, and on the 21st, joined the expedition which captured Fernandina, Fla., being the first regiment to land from the transports and the first to take possession of the town. It remained here until Jan. 17, 1863, when it returned to Hilton Head, and on June 24th went to St. Helena island as part of a force under Gen. Strong for the assault on Morris island, S. C., July 4 it went to Folly island, and on the 10th landed on Morris island, where it carried the enemy's rifle pits in front of their works. The regiment formed a part of the assaulting forces in the attacks on Fort Wagner, July 11 and 18, and Sept. 6. Its casualties in the several assaults were over 300 men in killed, wounded and missing. The 9th continued at Black and Morris islands, S. C., until April 18, 1864. In the meantime 416 of the original members reenlisted for an additional term of three years. In the spring of 1864 it was transferred to the Army of the Potomac and arrived at Gloucester Point, Va., April 22, where the reenlisted men, who had been home on 30 day furlough, rejoined the regiment on the 28th. It sailed up the James river on May 4 to Bermuda Hundred, and from this time on saw much hard service at the front, participating in the following engagements: Drewry's Bluff, Bermuda Hundred, losing 52 men; Cold Harbor, where its loss was over 70 men; the assaults on Petersburg; Deep Bottom, Fort Gilmer, Darbytown Road, losing 48 men. Oct. 28, it went to Chaffin's farm, and after the capture of Fort Fisher, N. C., in 1865, it was ordered there. Later it took possession of Wilmington, then joined Gen. Sherman's forces at Cox's bridge, after which it proceeded to Magnolia and from there to Raleigh, N. C., which city it entered April 11, 1865. It remained at Raleigh until July 13, 1865, when it was mustered out and proceeded to Augusta, Me., where the men were paid and finally discharged.

TENTH INFANTRY

Col., George L. Beal; Lieut.-Col., James F. Fillebrown; Majs., Charles Walker, Charles S. Emerson. When the 1st Me. was mustered out of service in the Union army the various companies composing it, and which had enlisted in the State militia for two years and in the U. S. service for only three months, were ordered to rendezvous at Portland for the purpose of reorganizing the regiment to serve out the rest of their time. This was found to be partially impracticable, however, except by the employment of coercive measures. All the companies were reorganized except A, C and D, but 697 out of the 881 men were paid bounty as newly enlisted troops. Co. C was formed by a fusion of the three companies not able to organize separately; Co. A was recruited in Saco, and Co. D was raised in Aroostook county. These companies were organized to form the new 10th at Cape Elizabeth, Me., in Oct., 1861, and were mustered into the U. S. service as follows: Companies B, C, E, F, G, H, I, and K to serve two years from May 3, 1861, and A and D to serve three years from Oct. 4, 1861.. The two years men were mustered out of service May 7 and 8, 1863, and the remaining men consolidated into a battalion of three companies, A, B and D, which was transferred to the 29th Me. on Nov. 1, 1863, by a special order from the war department. The regiment left Portland Oct. 6, 1861, and arrived in Baltimore on the 9th, where it remained encamped at "Patterson Park" until Nov. 4, when it moved to Relay House, Md., and relieved the 4th Wis. as guard of the Baltimore & Ohio railroad until Feb. 27, 1862. It afterward guarded the main line of the same road leading to Harper's Ferry, and the railroads leading to Martinsburg and Charlestown, W. Va. The regiment was concentrated at Winchester on May 24, and the following day was given the dangerous duty of rear-guard to the forces of Gen. Banks on his retreat to Williamsport, Md., during which it suffered a loss of 90 men. At Williamsport it was assigned to the 1st brigade, 1st division, Banks' corps. May 28, it made a reconnoissance towards Martinsburg, advanced to Winchester on the 31st, occupied Front Royal June 22, and took part in the reconnoissance to Luray Court House on June 29. On July 6, it proceeded towards Culpeper Court House and arrived there on the 24th. Gen. Crawford, the brigade commander, often stated that the 10th Me. contained more scouts than all other regiments in the brigade combined. It subsequently participated in the battle of Cedar mountain, where its losses were 173 men, and was in all the movements of Gen. Pope's army on his retreat toward Washington. At the battle of Antietam the regiment lost 20 killed and 48 wounded. From Sept. 19, 1862, to Sept. 28, 1863, it was at Maryland heights, opposite Harper's Ferry, Berlin, Md., Fairfax Station and Stafford Court House, Va., leaving the latter place on April 28, 1863, for Maine, as the two years' term of service had expired. The original members were mustered out at Portland on May 7-8, 1863. The three years' men were detached from the regiment on April 26, and organized into a battalion of three companies. On Sunday, April 26, 1863, the following order was received from corps headquarters: "Special Order No. 100. (extract) The enlisted men of the 10th Me. volunteers, whose term of service extends to three years or during the war, will be marched to these headquarters in charge of the following named officers: Capt. J. D. Beardsley, Lieut. Charles F. King, Lieut. Chandler Libbey, Lieut. Charles H. Haskell, and Ass't Surgeon H. N. Howard. These men will be constituted a provost guard, relieving the three companies of the 2nd Mass. volunteers now on duty at these headquarters. They will be allowed to retain their full proportion of camp and garrison equipage. By command of Maj.-Gen. Slocum."As soon as the battalion had reported, the officers and men referred to were immediately organized into three equal companies, and on April 29, with the rest of the 12th corps, crossed the Rappahannock and arrived at Chancellorsville on the 30th. It was not actively engaged in the battle which ensued here and lost only a few men. It next participated in every part of the campaign ending in the battle of Gettysburg, and was encamped along the Rappahannock and Rapidan rivers from Aug. 1 to Sept. 24, 1863, when it accompanied the 12th corps to Nashville, Tenn. From Nashville it went to Wartrace, and remained there until Nov. 1, 1863, when it was assigned to the 29th Me. infantry then being organized, and which the battalion joined at New Orleans, La.

Cols., John C. Caldwell, Harris M. Plaisted, Jonathan A. Hill; Lieut.-Cols., Harris M. Plaisted, William M. Shaw, Robert F. Campbell, Winslow P. Spofford, Jonathan A. Hill, Charles P. Baldwin; Majs., William M. Shaw, Robert F. Campbell, Winslow P. Spofford, Jonathan A. Hill, Charles P. Baldwin, Henry C. Adams. The ten preceding regiments had been raised at the expense of the state, under the act of the legislature of April 25, 1861, and the captains and subalterns of the organized companies elected the field officers. The 11th was the first to be raised at the direct expense of the general government, and the colonel, lieutenant-colonel and major were chosen before the companies were organized. The regiment was organized for active service Oct. 11, 1861, and mustered into the U. S. service on Nov. 12, to serve for three years. It left the state the next day for Washington, where it remained encamped until March 28, 1862, when, as part of Casey's division, it proceeded to Alexandria, thence to Newport News. Here on April 6 it was detached from its brigade (Naglee's), and went to the mouth of Warwick creek, where it was under the fire of the rebel gunboat Teazer. On the 17th, it rejoined the division and brigade and proceeded to Yorktown, where on the 29th it was in a sharp engagement with the enemy. Later it took a prominent part in the battles of Williamsburg, Seven Pines and White Oak swamp. From Aug. 16, to Dec. 26, 1862, it was at Yorktown, and on the latter date embarked with Naglee's brigade for Port Royal, S. C., where it landed on Feb. 10, 1863. Gen. Naglee, having been promoted to the command of a division, issued a spirited order on leaving the regiment, of which the following is a part: "Yours is the honor of having been the first to pass and the last to leave the Chickahominy. And, while you led the advance from this memorable place near Richmond, you were the last in the retreating column when, after seven days' constant fighting, it reached a place of security and rest at Harrison's Landing." The regiment remained in the South until April, 1864, during which time it participated in the unsuccessful attack on Charleston, and was engaged for a long time as artillerists, shelling Sumter and the Confederate works on Sullivan and James' islands. In April, 1864, it joined Gen. Butler's command at Gloucester Point, Va., and during the remainder of the war saw almost continuous fighting. On Nov. 2, 1864, about

130 of the men left the field for Maine, as their term of service had expired, and were mustered out at Augusta on Nov. 18. The next day, Nov., 3, the rest of the regiment went with Gen. Butler to New York to assist in maintaining order in that city at the presidential election, after which it returned to the front. The total casualties of the regiment during 1864 were 363, killed, wounded, missing and prisoners. It received 549 recruits, also a full company of volunteers—the 8th unassigned infantry. During the first three months of 1865, it formed a part of the 3d brigade, 1st division, 24th corps, and was stationed near the New Market road, 10 miles from Richmond. On March 27, it crossed the James and Appomattox rivers, engaged the enemy at Hatcher's run on the 31st, and was almost constantly exposed to the fire until April 2, losing meanwhile 3 enlisted men killed, 2 officers and several enlisted men wounded, and 1 officer and 15 enlisted men captured. It participated in the assault and capture of Forts Gregg and Baldwin, losing 25 enlisted men killed and wounded, and on the 3d moved with the army in pursuit of Lee's forces. At "Clover Hill" on the 9th, it lost 6 enlisted men killed, 2 officers and 29 enlisted men wounded. It remained in the vicinity of Richmond until Nov. 24, and on the 26th, moved to Fredericksburg, where it remained, doing patrol and other duties until the middle of Jan., 1866, when it was ordered to City Point, Va., to be mustered out. It was mustered out on Feb. 2, 1866, in accordance with orders of the war department, and left on the 3d for Augusta, Me., where the men were paid and finally discharged. The regiment saw an unusual amount of hard service, and left a splendid name for intrepidity and heroism.

TWELFTH INFANTRY

Cols., George F. Shepley, William K. Kimball; Lieut.-Cols., William K. Kimball, Edwin Illsley; Majs., David R. Hastings, Gideon A. Hastings. This regiment was organized at Portland, Nov. 16, 1861, to serve for three years, and was mustered out of service at the same place, Dec. 7, 1864, the recruits and reenlisted men, however, being organized into a battalion of four companies and remaining in the field. This battalion was afterwards ordered to Savannah, Ga., and was raised to a full regiment by the assignment of the 10th, 11th, 15th, 18th, and 16th, companies of unassigned infantry, organized at Augusta, Me., in the early part of 1865, to serve, one, two and three years, and which were assigned as Companies E, F, G, H, I and K, respectively. The regiment was intended from the outset to form a part of Gen. Butler's New England division, designed for the capture of New Orleans. It left the state for Lowell, Mass., on Nov. 24, 1861, and after a delay of several weeks at Lowell and Fortress Monroe, finally disembarked at Ship island, Miss. On May 4, 1862, the regiment went to New Orleans, which city had fallen into Union hands, and where Col. Shepley, now commanding the 3d brigade of Gen. Butler's army was appointed military commandant of the city. The regiment saw much exciting and arduous service in the South before it finally returned to the battlefields of Virginia, on July 20, 1864. Col. Kimball, who succeeded Col. Shepley in command of the regiment, aided by a gunboat, performed brilliant service at Manchac pass, where he captured two Confederate batteries of six 32-pounders, with a stand of colors, a large amount of stores, and $8000 of Confederate currency. The achievement was eulogized by the war department, which ordered the captured colors to be kept in the possession of the 12th and they were subsequently added to the trophies of the state. The 12th, during this period, also took an important part in the reduction of Port Hudson, accompanied the expedition of Gen. Grover up Grand lake, and engaged the enemy at Donaldsonville, La. On March 12, 1864, two-thirds of the regiment reenlisted as veterans, and went back to Maine on a short furlough. They rejoined the regiment at New Orleans on June 16. On the arrival of the regiment at Fortress Monroe on July 20, 1864, it reported to Gen. Butler at Bermuda Hundred. From this time until the muster out it was engaged in an almost incessant conflict. It participated in the battle of Winchester, where it lost 113 officers and men; at Cedar creek it lost 82 officers and men, and was in many smaller engagements. On Nov. 19, 1864, the term of service of about 80 of the officers and men having expired, they returned to Maine and were mustered out. The recruits and reenlisted men, augmented by unassigned infantry, as above detailed, remained in the field to form a new regiment. The two and three years' men remained on duty, together with the battalion of veterans, at Savannah, Ga., until April 18, 1866, when the whole battalion was mustered out of service at that place.

THIRTEENTH INFANTRY

Cols., Neal Dow, Henry Rust, Jr.; Lieut.-Cols., Henry Rust, Jr., Frank S. Hasseltine; Majs., Frank S. Hasseltine, Abernethy Grover. The 13th regiment was raised at large, and rendezvoused at Augusta. It was mustered into service for three years on Dec. 13, 1861, and left Feb. 18, 1862, for Boston, where it embarked on board transports for Ship island, Miss., arriving there in March. During its long stay on Ship island, it suffered severely in health, though it excelled in drill and discipline. Detachments of the regiment were sent into the defenses of New Orleans, July 5, 1862, and the entire regiment was ordered there on Sept. 1. The 13th remained in the South until July 1, 1864, when it was ordered north and arrived at Fortress Monroe on the 12th. While in the South it participated in the capture of Point Isabel, Tex., Mustang island, and of Fort Esperanza, commanding Pass Caballo, the entrance to Matagorda bay. In April, 1864, it formed part of the Red River expedition under Gen. Banks, and was in the battle of Pleasant Hill, La. Soon after its arrival in the North, it went to Harper's Ferry. On Aug. 3, 1864, the reenlisted men proceeded to Maine on furlough, and rejoined the regiment at Harper's Ferry on Oct. 1. As communication with the front was impossible at this time, Gen. Stephenson on the 5th ordered the regiment to Martinsburg, W. Va., to strengthen the defenses of that place, as it was the base of supplies for Sheridan's whole army. Here the regiment remained engaged in picket and patrol duty until the expiration of their original term of service. The original members who had not reenlisted arrived in Augusta, Dec. 30, 1864 and were mustered out at that place on Jan. 6, 1865. Two hundred and fifty-two reenlisted men and 82 recruits, whose term of service had not expired, transferred to and consolidated with the 30th regiment of infantry, Maine volunteers.

FOURTEENTH INFANTRY

Cols., Frank S. Nickerson, Thomas W. Porter, Albion K. Bolan; Lieut.-Cols., Elias Milliken, Thomas W. Porter, Charles S. Bickmore, Albion K. Bolan, John K. Laing; Majs., Thomas W. Porter, Charles S. Bickmore, Albion K. Bolan, John K. Laing, Joseph M. Wiswell. This regiment, like all those raised in 1861 at the expense of the general government, was recruited from the state at large. It was organized at Augusta, from Dec. 3 to Dec. 17, 1861, to serve for three years, and left the state for Boston Feb. 5, 1862. It sailed at once from there for Ship island, Miss., where it arrived on March 8, and remained in the South until July 13, 1864, during which time it saw an unusual amount of trying and dangerous service. Its first serious engagement was at Baton Rouge, Aug. 5, 1862, where it lost in killed, wounded and missing 126 men. Other engagements in which they participated were at St. Charles Court House, Civiques ferry, and the assaults on the fortifications of Port Hudson, May 27, and June 14, 1863. During the campaign from May 7 to Aug. 5 of this year, the regiment was without tents of any kind, and their only camp equipage was their camp-kettles. Both officers and men were forced to sleep in the open air, and they suffered much from chills and fever. In Jan., 1864, all but 40 of the available men of the regiment reenlisted for an additional term of three years, and on Feb. 10 they left New Orleans for Maine on a furlough of 30 days. They rejoined the regiment at New Orleans May 19, 1864. On the arrival of the 14th at Bermuda Hundred, Va., July 22, 1864, it was at once assigned to Gen. Butler's command. Joining Gen. Sheridan's forces at Berryville, Va., on the 18th, it took an important part in the battle of Winchester on Sept. 19, losing 60 killed, wounded and prisoners, or about one-third of the number engaged. Subsequently it participated in the assault and capture of Fisher's hill and joined in the pursuit of Gen. Early to Harrisonburg. At the battle of Cedar creek it again suffered severe losses. Of the 200 men in the 14th who entered this fight, 80 were either killed, wounded or captured, Lieut.-Col. Bickmore being among the killed. Shortly after this battle the regiment moved to a position near Kernstown, where it remained until the expiration of its term of service, Dec. 23, 1864. The original members who had not reenlisted were mustered out at Augusta, Me., on Jan. 13, 1865. The reenlisted men and recruits whose term of service had not expired, were organized into a battalion of four companies, A, B, C and D. The 13th, 14th, 17th, 20th, 22nd and 23d companies unassigned infantry, organized in Augusta in April, 1865, to serve one year, were assigned to this battalion as Companies E, F, G, H, I and K, thereby reorganizing the battalion into a full regiment. The new regiment was variously stationed at Savannah, Augusta and Darien, Ga., engaged in guard and patrol duty, until Aug. 28, 1865, when the entire regiment was mustered out. On Sept. 1 it embarked for Maine, and the men were finally paid and discharged at Augusta on Sept. 28.

FIFTEENTH INFANTRY

Cols., John McCluskey, Isaac Dyer; Lieut.-Cols., Isaac Dyer, Benjamin B. Murray, Jr., Pembroke; Majs., Benjamin Hawes, Franklin M. Drew, James H. Whitmore, John R. Coates. This regiment was raised principally in Aroostock county, and was organized at Augusta, Me., from Dec. 6 to 31, 1861, to serve for three years. It was mustered into the U. S. service on Jan. 23, 1862, and embarked from Portland March 6 for Ship island, Miss., at which date it numbered 962 men, rank and file. The regiment remained encamped at Carrollton, La., from May 19 to Sept. 18, during which time it suffered much from malarial diseases. In September it went to Pensacola, Fla., where it remained until June 21, 1863. Here the health of the men so improved that the number in hospital was reduced to less than one-quarter. During the first year of its service the 15th lost by desertion, discharge and death 329 men, although it had never been in battle. On its return to New Orleans in June, 1863, it joined Gen. Banks' expedition to Texas and rendered conspicuous service in the capture of Fort Esperanza, in Matagorda bay. While at Matagorda peninsula, from Jan. 17 to Feb. 28, 1864, three-fourths of the original members of the regiment reenlisted for another term of three years. Returning to New Orleans in March, the regiment formed a part of Gen. Banks' Red river expedition, during which it marched more than 700 miles in two months, and participated in the battles of Sabine cross-roads, Pleasant Hill, Cane river crossing and Mansura plains. In June, 1864, it was ordered to New Orleans, and on July 5 embarked on transports for Fortress Monroe, Va., where it arrived on the 17th. Six companies were then ordered to Bermuda Hundred, and the remaining companies participated in the campaign up the valley in pursuit of Early's army. The command was reunited at Monocacy Junction, Md., Aug. 4, when the veterans of the regiment who had reenlisted received a 35 days' furlough, returning to the field Sept. 27. In October it went to Martinsburg, where it remained until Jan. 7, 1865. The original members of the regiment who had not reenlisted were mustered out on Jan. 18, 1865, but the reenlisted men, recruits, volunteers, drafted men and substitutes forwarded from Camp Berry, Portland, were sufficient to reorganize the regiment, which was ordered to Washington in April, and went to Savannah, Ga., on June 4. On the 13th, it embarked on transports for Georgetown, S. C., where it was assigned to the 3d separate brigade, Department of South Carolina, and remained here until the date of muster out, July 5, 1866, whence the men went to New York, where they were finally paid and discharged.

SIXTEENTH INFANTRY

Cols., Asa W. Wildes, Charles W. Tilden; Lieut.-Cols., Charles W. Tilden, Augustus B. Farnham; Majs., Augustus B. Farnham, Archibald D. Leavitt, Abner R. Small. The recruits for this regiment were rendezvoused at Augusta during the months of May, June and July, and the regiment was mustered into the U. S. service on Aug. 14, 1862, to serve for three years. The regiment left for Washington on the 19th with 38 commissioned officers and 944 enlisted men, and remained encamped there until Sept. 7, when it proceeded to Rappahannock Station as a part of Taylor's brigade, Hooker's corps. Here it was transferred to Duryea's brigade of Reynolds' corps. It had left camp at Fort Tillinghast, near Washington, in light marching order and during the next two months the men suffered terribly from the lack of sufficient clothing and camp equipage. By the middle of October the regiment had dwindled to less than 700 men, and of these 250 were at one time on the sick list. Even medicines for the sick were lacking and the hardships endured by these men, so recently taken from the peaceful walks of life, can never be told. Finally, at the end of October, they drew shoes and shelter tents, Nov. 27 (Thanksgiving day), their knapsacks and overcoats arrived from Washington. The self-respect of the men was now restored and a better feeling took the place of the old despondency. The loss the regiment suffered in its first serious battle tells the story of its valor. About 450 men were engaged at Fredericksbtirg on Dec. 13, 1862, and 226 of this number was either killed, wounded or missing. Said Gen. Burnside, who commanded that day: "Whatever honor we can claim in that contest was won by Maine men."

The regiment again lost heavily at Gettysburg, when, at the close of the terrible three days' fighting, all that remained of 248 officers and men, who entered the battle, were 2 officers and 15 enlisted men. Besides the battles above mentioned, the list of engagements in which this regiment bore an honorable part would include, Chancellorsville, Mine Run, Wilderness, Spottsylvania Court House, where it lost nearly 100 men, Laurel Hill, losing nearly 50 men, North Anna river, Totopotomy, Bethesda Church, Petersburg, Weldon railroad, Hatcher's run, losing 3 killed, 60 wounded and 11 missing, Gravelly run, losing 29 men, and the South Side railroad. It joined in the pursuit of Lee's forces to Appomattox Court House, after which it returned to Washington, D. C, where it was mustered out on June 5, 1865, and the next day the men were en route for the state rendezvous at Augusta where they were finally paid and discharged. The regiment had received about 800 recruits and in addition the 2nd company of unassigned infantry, organized at Augusta, Me., Sept. 23, 1864, to serve for one year, joined the regiment and was assigned as Co. A. The officers and men whose term of service did not expire before Oct. 1, 1865, were transferred to the 20th Me.

SEVENTEENTH INFANTRY

Cols., Thomas A. Roberts, George W. West, Charles P. Mattocks; Lieut-Cols., Charles B. Merrill, William Hobson; Majs., George W. West, Charles P. Mattocks. This regiment was recruited chiefly from the counties of York, Cumberland, Androscoggin and Oxford, and was mustered into the U. S. service at Camp King, Cape Elizabeth, Aug. 18, 1862, to serve for three years. On June 4, 1864, 129 of the recruits of the 3d Me., whose term of service had not expired on the date of the muster-out of that command, were transferred to the 17th. The war department also directed on Feb. 1, 1865, the transfer to this regiment of Co. D, 2nd U. S. sharpshooters. The members of the regiment whose term of service expired prior to Oct. 1, 1865, were mustered out at Bailey's cross-roads, June 4, 1865, and the remaining men were transferred to the 1st Me. heavy artillery. The 17th left the state for Washington Aug. 21, 1862, and occupied the line of forts on the east side of the Anacosta and north side of the Potomac rivers, until Oct. 7, engaged in both heavy artillery and infantry drill and garrison duty. It then joined the 3d brigade (Berry's), 1st division (Birney's), 3d corps, at Upton's hill, Va. On Dec. 13, 1862, it participated in the battle of Fredericksburg, losing 2 men killed and 19 wounded, and was complimented by Gen. Berry for the steadiness of the men, who were under fire for the first time. The regiment remained encamped at Falmouth, Va., until May 1, 1863, when it took part in the Chancellorsville campaign, being hotly engaged at Chancellorsville on May 2-3, losing 113 men in killed, wounded and missing out of about 625 men in the action. The regiment was next engaged at Gettysburg, during the last two days of the battle, where it lost 132 in killed, wounded and missing. On Nov. 27, it took a prominent part in the battle of Orange Grove, losing 52 men. It wintered at Brandy Station until March 25, 1864, during which time its ranks were filled by returned convalescents and recruits, and numbered about 500 men for the spring campaign. It was now assigned to the 2nd brigade, 3d division, 2nd army corps, and participated in the battle of the Wilderness, losing 24 men killed, 147 wounded and 12 missing. On the 12th, the corps made its famous charge upon the enemy's lines at the Po river, where the regiment lost 53 men, and on the 23d, in the charge which drove the enemy across the North Anna river, it lost 23 men. It was under fire at Cold Harbor, and in two assaults on the enemy's works at Petersburg it lost 84 men. Subsequently it encamped near Fort Sedgwick, where it remained until Feb. 5, 1865, having meanwhile taken part in the attack on the Weldon railroad under Gen. Warren. They subsequently participated in all the movements of the 2nd corps in the vicinity of Hatcher's run, until March 29, 1865. On May 1, it left Burkesville, Va., for Washington, where it was mustered out on June 4. Its aggregate losses during the years 1862, 1863 and 1864 were 745.

EIGHTEENTH INFANTRY

Col., Daniel Chaplin; Lieut.-Col., Thomas H. Talbot; Maj., Charles Hamlin. The regiment was raised chiefly in the Penobscot valley, and was mustered into the U. S. service at Bangor, Aug. 21, 1862, to serve for three years. It left the state on Aug. 24 for Washington, where, after doing duty in the defenses of the capital on the Virginia side for nearly five months, the organization was changed to heavy artillery by order of the war department of Dec. 19, 1862, and was numbered the 1st regiment heavy artillery, Maine volunteers.

NINETEENTH INFANTRY

Cols., Frederick D. Sewell, Francis E. Heath, Selden Connor, James W. Welch, Isaac W. Starbird; Lieut.-Cols., Francis E. Heath, Henry W. Cunningham, Isaac W. Starbird, Joseph W. Spaulding; Majs., Henry W. Cunningham, James W. Welch, Isaac W. Starbird, Joseph W. Spaulding, David E. Parsons. A large portion of the men in the 19th came from Sagadahoc, Waldo, Knox and Kennebec counties and the regiment was mustered into the U. S. service at Bath, Aug. 25, 1862, to serve for three years. On the 27th it left for Washington, numbering 39 officers and 969 enlisted men, having been raised, organized and equipped in less than four weeks. It remained in garrison at Washington until the end of September, when it went to Harper's Ferry, and was assigned to the 1st brigade, 2nd division, 2nd corps. During a reconnaissance in force Oct. 16, to Charlestown, it was under fire for the first time, the men behaving with the coolness which ever afterwards characterized the regiment. During its term of service, it saw an unusual amount of active duty, and, in addition to innumerable skirmishes, was engaged in the battles at Fredericksburg, Chancellorsville, Bristoe Station, Gettysburg, the Wilderness, Mine run, Spottsylvania Court House, Po river, Totopotomy, North Anna river, Bethesda Church, Cold Harbor, Petersburg, Deep Bottom, Reams' station, Strawberry Plains, Hatcher's run, Boydton plank road, Fort Powell, Amelia Springs and High bridge. At Gettysburg it went into action with 440 officers and men and lost during two days 12 officers and 220 enlisted men. Its losses were also very severe at the battle of the Wilderness, on the Jerusalem plank road, and in front of Petersburg. It was exposed to the fire of artillery and sharpshooters in the immediate front of Petersburg both night and day, from Oct. 20 to 26, 1864. Its casualties during the year 1864 were as follows: killed in action, 61; wounded, 16 officers, 283 men; captured, 1 officer, 133 men. On June 18, 1864, 277 men were transferred to this regiment from the 4th Me. infantry, and on Oct. 22, 1864, the 5th unassigned Me. infantry, organized at Augusta, Oct. 4, 1864, to serve one, two and three years, joined this regiment. On May 2, 1865, it left Burkesville, Va., for Washington, and was mustered out on May 31 at Bailey's cross-roads. The officers and men whose term of service did not expire prior to Oct. 1, 1865, were transferred to the 1st Me. heavy artillery.

TWENTIETH INFANTRY

Cols., Adelbert Ames, Joshua L. Chamberlain, Charles D. Gilmore, Ellis Spear; Lieut.-Cols., Joshua L. Chamberlain, Charles D. Gilmore, Walter G. Morrill, Thomas D. Chamberlain; Majs., Charles D. Gilmore, Ellis Spear, Atherton W. Clark, George R Abbott. This was the last of the three-year regiments raised in the state in the summer of 1862. It was rendezvoused at Portland and mustered into the U. S. service Aug. 29, 1862. The original members whose term of service expired prior to Oct. 1, 1865, were mustered out at Washington, D. C., June 5, 1865, and the enlisted men of the 16th Me. infantry and the 1st Me. sharpshooters were transferred to the 20th, June 5 and June 21, 1865, respectively. The regiment as thus reorganized was finally mustered out near Washington, July 16, 1865. On Sept. 3, 1862, the 20th left the state, and on the 7th went into camp at the arsenal grounds, Washington, D. C. Attached to Butterfield's brigade, Porter's division, it formed a portion of the reserve at Antietam, and was under fire for 36 hours at the battle of Fredericksburg, where the men acted with great gallantry in this, their first serious battle. A list of the important battles in which the 20th subsequently engaged includes Chancellorsville, Gettysburg, Rappahannock Station, Mine Run, Wilderness, Spottsylvania, Totopotomy, North Anna river, Bethesda Church, Hatcher's run, Petersburg, Weldon railroad, Peebles' farm, Boydton road, Gravelly run and Five Forks. After the battle of Chancellorsville, Col. Ames was promoted to brigadier-general, and Lieut.-Col. Chamberlain assumed command. Under his command it formed the extreme left of the line at Gettysburg on the second day of that sanguinary contest and was hotly engaged for many hours. Its total loss was 3 officers and 134 enlisted men killed and wounded. At the opening of the spring campaign of 1864, recruits and re-

52

turning convalescents augmented the numbers of the regiment about l00 men, so that it numbered 347 muskets. It was still attached to the 3d brigade, 1st division, 5th corps. On June 6, 1864, Col. Chamberlain was assigned to the command of the 1st brigade of the division and Maj. Spear assumed command of the regiment. In the gallant charge on the enemy's works at Peebles' farm on Sept. 30, 1864, it suffered a loss of 57 men killed and wounded, out of 167 men taken into action, but captured 6 commissioned officers, 70 men and a piece of artillery. Its whole number of casualties during the year 1864 was 298; and it received 200 recruits. In Jan., 1865, it mustered 275 muskets for duty. On the completion of negotiations for the surrender of Lee's army, the 20th was one of the regiments designated to receive the Confederate arms.

TWENTY-FIRST INFANTRY

Col., Elijah D. Johnson; Lieut-Col., Nathan Stanley; Maj., Benjamin G. Merry. This regiment, like the seven succeeding ones, was raised under the call of Aug. 4, 1862, for 300,000 militia for nine months' service. It was mustered into the U. S. service at Bangor, Oct. 14, 1862, and started for Washington, D. C., on the 21st. While en route it was ordered to report to Maj.-Gen. N. P. Banks, commanding the Department of the Gulf, at New York city, then organizing his expedition for the opening of the Mississippi. It remained quartered at East New York for two months and then proceeded to New Orleans, where it arrived early in Feb., 1863. It went at once to Baton Rouge and was assigned to the 1st brigade, 1st division, 19th corps. The men suffered from disease contracted in the low southern country, despite the utmost precautions taken. Baton Rouge was now an important Union "base," and the regiment was occupied in doing picket duty and protecting the city from guerrilla attacks. On March 14th, it advanced with the corps against Port Hudson, while Adm. Farragut's fleet was engaged in passing the enemy's works there on that memorable night. The army, however, made no attack in force at that time, but on May 21 it engaged the enemy at Plains Store. The regiment took part in the siege of Port Hudson and participated in the assaults on May 27 and June 14, losing in the two engagements 88 men killed and wounded. Though its term of service had expired during the siege, the regiment volunteered to remain until the capture of Port Hudson, which occurred on July 9, 1863. Preparations were then at once made to transport home those regiments that had already remained beyond their term of service. The 20th was assigned to the 2nd brigade of the post forces, and July 25 embarked for Maine. With other regiments, it was the first to pass up the Mississippi river and received a continuous ovation. It arrived in Augusta, Aug. 7, where the men were mustered out on Aug. 25th, by Lieut. F. E. Crossman of the 17th U. S infantry.

TWENTY-SECOND INFANTRY

Col., Simon G. Jerrard; Lieut.-Col., Olonzo G. Putnam; Maj., John O. Brackett. This regiment was rendezvoused at Camp John Pope, Bangor, and was mustered into service Oct. 18, 1862, to serve nine months. It left on the 21st for Washington, where it arrived on the 24th and remained encamped at Arlington Heights until Nov. 3, when it was temporarily assigned to the 3d brigade, Casey's division, commanded by Col. Fessenden, of the 25th Me. Having been ordered to Fortress Monroe to form a part of the projected expedition to New Orleans, it embarked Dec. 4 at Newport News and arrived at New Orleans on the 15th. On the 17th it occupied Baton Rouge and was assigned to the 1st brigade, Grover's division. It participated in the reconnaissance in the rear of Port Hudson March 13 to 16, and on March 26 formed a part of the expedition up the Atchafalaya to attack the enemy's works in the rear. It defeated the enemy in a sharp engagement at Irish bend on April 14, and garrisoned at Franklin until the 25th, when it went to New Iberia. On May 6, it moved toward Port Hudson, where it arrived on June 1, having marched over 500 miles during the campaign. It participated in two assaults on the works at Port Hudson, June 9 and 14, and after the surrender of that place was quartered inside the works until July 24, when it started for Maine, going by boat to Cairo, Ill., thence by rail to Bangor, where it arrived on Aug. 6, and was mustered out on the 15th.

TWENTY-THIRD INFANTRY

Col., William Wirt Virgin; Lieut.-Col., Enos T. Luce; Maj., Alfred B. Soule. This regiment was entirely composed of men from the counties of Androscoggin and Oxford, except one company from Cumberland county. Many of its members were graduates of seminaries and colleges and the moral and intellectual qualities of the men were of an exceptionally high order. They went into camp at Portland, and were there mustered in on Sept. 29, 1862, for nine months. The regiment left for Washington Oct. 18, arrived there on the 20th, and on the 25th received orders to report to Gen. Grover at Seneca, Md., where it was assigned the duty of guarding the several fords of the upper Potomac. It performed this duty with care and fidelity until May 24, 1863, when it was ordered to Alexandria, Va., and was there engaged for several weeks in digging rifle-pits, building barricades across the principal streets and patrolling the town, in addition to sending out a large number of men daily for Picket duty. On June 17, it moved back to Poolsville, Md., and to Maryland heights opposite Harper's Ferry on the 24th. On the 27th, it was ordered to Portland, Me., where the men were discharged on July 15. During its ten months' of service, it lost about 50 men by disease, and 2 by accident. By the fortunes of war it was never under fire, but this was no fault of the officers or men, who established a good reputation among all with whom they came in contact for good order, sobriety and excellent discipline.

TWENTY-FOURTH INFANTRY

Col., George M. Atwood; Lieut.-Cols., Charles T. Bean, Eben Hutchinson; Majs., Eben Hutchinson, William Holbrook. This regiment was mustered into the U. S. service at Augusta, Oct. 16, 1862, to serve for nine months. On the 20th it left for New York and reported to Maj.-Gen. Banks. The regiment was detained at East New York by sickness until Jan. 12, 1863, when it embarked for New Orleans, arriving there Feb. 14. On the 26th it was ordered to Bonnet Carre, 40 miles above New Orleans, and was there assigned to the 3d brigade, 2nd division, under command of Gen. Nickerson. While at this place details from the regiment were variously engaged in active duties at different times and places. On May 21, it was ordered to Port Hudson and participated in the entire siege of that stronghold, including the desperate assaults of May 27 and June 14, but suffered few casualties. The southern climate, however, worked havoc in their ranks, as they lost 184 men from disease and nearly 100 more were discharged for disability. Of the 900 men who went out with the regiment, 570 returned. It left Port Hudson for Maine, via Cairo, Ill., July 24, arrived at Augusta on Aug. 6, and was mustered out on the 25th of the same month, after a term of service of nearly one year. None was killed in battle or died of wounds.

TWENTY-FIFTH INFANTRY

Col., Francis Fessenden; Lieut.-Col., Charles E. Shaw; Maj., Alexander M. Tolman. This regiment was mustered into the U. S. service at Portland, Sept. 29, 1862, to serve for nine months. It comprised 993 men, and left for Washington on Oct. 13, arriving in that city on the 18th. It was assigned to the 3d brigade, Casey's division, Reserve army corps, for the defense of the national capital, and remained encamped on Arlington Heights, on the north side of Columbia turnpike, in front of the line of defenses from Oct. 26, 1862, to March 24, 1863, continually engaged in guarding "Long Bridge" and constructing fortifications. On March 24, 1863, it was ordered to Chantilly, Va., on the Little River turnpike, and remained on picket duty in that vicinity until June 26, when it was ordered back to Arlington Heights. On June 30, it started for Maine and arrived July 3 at Portland, where the men were mustered out of the U. S. service July 10. During its term of service the regiment participated in no engagements, but faithfully performed every duty assigned it. The losses were 25 men who died of disease; 5 officers and 27 men discharged; 13 deserted, and 9 were transferred.

TWENTY-SIXTH INFANTRY

Col., Nathaniel H. Hubbard; Lieut.-Col., Philo Hersey; Maj., James N. Fowler. This regiment was raised in the counties of Knox, Hancock and Waldo, and was rendezvoused at Camp John

Pope, Bangor, where it was mustered into the U. S. service Oct. 11. 1862, to serve for three years. It left the state Oct. 23, and arrived in Washington on the 27th. On Nov. 9 it embarked for Fortress Monroe, and on Dec. 1 reembarked at Newport News on the steamers Pocahontas and Matanzas for Ship island, where it arrived on the 12th, and at New Orleans on the 16th. It proceeded at once to Baton Rouge, where it was assigned to the 3d brigade, Grover's division, remaining here until March 12. 1863, when it joined in the reconnaissance to Port Hudson, returning on the 16th, and on the 28th embarked on the river steamer St. Maurice for Donaldsonville, 60 miles below. Thence, with the other forces from Baton Rouge, it proceeded to Thibodeaux, thence by rail to Brashear City, and on April 11, together with Grover's division, it proceeded to Irish bend, near Franklin, La., where on the 14th it engaged the enemy and met with a loss of 68 men out of 300 engaged. On May 30 it arrived at Port Hudson and engaged in supporting a battery until June 14, when it participated in the assault of that day, afterward returning to its former position. On the surrender of Port Hudson, it remained on duty inside the fortifications until July 26, when it embarked for Maine, and was mustered out of the U. S. service at Bangor on Aug. 9. The mortality of the regiment from all causes was about 200.

TWENTY-SEVENTH INFANTRY

Cols., Rufus P. Tapley, Mark F. Wentworth; Lieut.-Cols., Mark F. Wentworth, James M. Stone; Majs., James M. Stone, John D. Hill. Most of the members of this regiment came from York county and were rendezvoused at Portland, where the regiment was mustered into service Sept. 30, 1862, to serve for nine months. They left on Oct. 20 for Washington, arriving there on the 22nd. On the 26th it marched to Arlington Heights, where it remained doing picket duty until Dec. 12th, when it was ordered to the south of Hunting creek. Here it relieved a Vermont brigade in the duty of guarding a picket line 8 miles long, extending from the Potomac near Mount Vernon to the Orange & Alexandria railroad, and remained here in the performance of that duty throughout a severe winter until March 24, 1863. It then moved to Chantilly, Va., doing picket duty on the outermost line of infantry in the defenses of Washington. On June 25 it returned to Arlington Heights. The term of service of the regiment had already expired, but 315 of the officers and men volunteered to remain and if necessary assist in the defense of the capital against the forces of Gen. Lee, who had then commenced his great invasion of Pennsylvania. On July 4, after the result of the battle of Gettysburg was announced, the regiment left for Maine and arrived at Portland on the 6th, where the men were mustered out on the 17th. The 27th left the state with 949 men, and lost 82 men by death, discharge and resignation.

TWENTY-EIGHTH INFANTRY

Col., Ephraim W. Woodman; Lieut.-Col., William E. Hadlock; Maj., Joseph D. Bullen. This regiment, numbering 935 men, was organized on Oct. 6, 1862, and was mustered into the U. S. service at Augusta, Oct. 18, to serve for nine months. On the 26th it left the state for Washington, but stopped en route at New York, and was ordered to Fort Schuyler to report to Gen. Banks. On Nov. 26 it was ordered to East New York, and on Jan. 17, 1863, embarked for Fortress Monroe and New Orleans, arriving at the latter place on the 29th. It encamped at Chalmette, 7 miles below the city, until Feb. 15, when it was ordered to Pensacola, Fla. On March 29 it returned to New Orleans, and was at once ordered to Donaldsonville and Plaquemine. On May 27, six companies under Col. Woodman were ordered to Port Hudson, and assigned to Gen. Nickerson's brigade of Dwight's division. They shared in the advance of June 14, and on June 22 assaulted a bastion of the Confederate works, losing 3 killed and 9 wounded. Meanwhile, the portion of the regiment which had remained at Donaldsonville to garrison Fort Butler, was attacked by a vastly superior force of the enemy, but repulsed them with heavy loss in one of the most gallant engagements of the war. The little garrison killed, captured and wounded more than three times its number, and was mentioned for gallantry in general orders read to the troops before Port Hudson. On July 4, the six companies at Port Hudson were ordered to Fort Butler, then besieged by the enemy, and arrived there on the 5th. The same evening, Maj. Bullen, who had so recently won distinction for his brilliant defense of the fort with his little command, was foully murdered by private Francis G. Scott of the 1st La. infantry. Owing to a dearth of field officers, Col. Woodward had been retained at Port Hudson. After the surrender of that place on the 8th he again took command of the regiment on the 10th and two days later took command of the post at Baton Rouge, where the regiment was stationed until Aug. 6, when it started for Maine via Cairo, Ill., arrived at Augusta on the 18th, and on the 31st was mustered out at that point. Many of the men had reenlisted while in the South, but all the men captured had been paroled or exchanged, and were mustered out with the others.

TWENTY-NINTH INFANTRY

Cols., George L. Beal, George H. Nye; Lieut.-Col., Charles S. Emerson; Majs., William Knowlton, George H. Nye, John M. Gould. Col. Beal, formerly of the 10th Me., was authorized to recruit this regiment, which was one of the veteran volunteer organizations raised in Maine near the close of 1863. It was organized at Augusta, from Nov. 13, 1863, to Jan., 1864, to serve for three years, with the exception of Companies A and D, which were transferred from the 10th Me. battalion and joined the regiment at New Orleans, La. Co. A was mustered out Oct. 18, 1864, its term of service having expired, and its place was filled by the 1st company of unassigned infantry, organized at Augusta on Sept. 1, 1864, to serve for one year. The new Co. A was mustered out June 5, 1865; the balance of the regiment was mustered out at Hilton Head, S. C., June 21, 1866, and arrived in New York harbor June 28, where the men were paid and discharged. The regiment left Augusta Jan. 31, 1864, and embarked at Portland on Feb. 2, on the steamship De Molay for New Orleans, where it arrived on the 16th. It participated in the Red River expedition under Gen. Banks, being assigned to the 1st brigade, 1st division, 19th corps, and rendered brilliant service at the battles of Mansfield and Pleasant Hill, La. It assisted in building the dam which saved the gunboats of the fleet, and was at one time without sleep and very little to eat for 60 hours, marching 56 miles in the meantime and fighting two battles. On July 12, it returned to Fortress Monroe and subsequently took part in all the movements of the Army of the Shenandoah, including the battles of Winchester, Fisher's hill, and Cedar creek. Maj. Knowlton was fatally wounded at Winchester, and in the action at Cedar creek the regiment lost 18 killed and in wounded. During the winter of 1864-65 it was in winter quarters in the neighborhood of Stephenson's depot, Va., attached to the 1st brigade, 1st division, 19th corps. It did guard duty at Washington arsenal over the assassins of President Lincoln on May 4-5, 1865, and took part in the grand review of the Army of the Potomac on the 23d. On June 5 it arrived in Savannah, Ga., by boat, whence they went to Georgetown, S. C., on the 14th and 15th. From this time until March 27, 1866, detachments of the regiment were occupied at various stations in South Carolina, with headquarters at Darlington. On the last-named date the regiment was ordered to Hilton Head, S. C., which it occupied, with detachments at St. Helena island and at Seabrook, until it was mustered out.

THIRTIETH INFANTRY

Cols., Francis Fessenden, Thomas H. Hubbard, Royal E. Whitman; Lieut.-Cols., Thomas H. Hubbard, Royal E. Whitman, George W. Randall; Majs., Royal E. Whitman, George W. Randall, Horace C. Haskell. Like many of the regiments formed in the latter years of the war, the 30th had a large number of experienced soldiers among its officers and men, though it also had some who were attracted by the large bounties offered and some who were old and disabled. The regiment was mustered in at Augusta from Dec. 12, 1863, to Jan. 8, 1864, to serve for three years. On Jan. 8, 1865, it was joined by three companies made up from the enlisted men of the 13th Me., whose term of service had not expired at the date of the muster out of that regiment, and were assigned to this organization on Nov. 18, 1864. The entire regiment was mustered out on Aug. 20, 1865, at Savannah, Ga. On Feb. 7, 1864, the 30th embarked at Portland on the steamer Merrimac for New Orleans, La., arriving there on the 16th. It participated in the Red River campaign as a part of the 3d brigade, 1st division, 19th corps, and took an honorable part in the battles of Sabine cross-roads and Pleasant Hill on April 8 and 9, respectively. It lost in the two engagements 11 killed, 66 wounded and 71 missing, and during the retreat of the Union forces to the Mississippi river, it took the most prominent part in the dislodgment of the enemy at Cane river crossing, which was perhaps the most gallant action of the disastrous campaign. Its loss here was 2 officers and 10 men killed, 2 officers and 67 men wounded, and 7 men missing. Soon after the close of this campaign, the regiment was sent north to Virginia. In August and the early part of September it moved with the Army of the Shenandoah, but did not share in the battles and victories of Gen. Sheridan in September and October, as the brigade was detached from its division until Oct. 26. On Nov. 9, 1864, it took up a position between Kernstown and Newton, and on Dec. 30 went into winter quarters at Stephenson's depot, 4 miles north of Winchester, but a few days later moved to Winchester. After the recruits from the 13th Me. joined the regiment at Winchester it was formed into seven companies and retained its field and staff officers without change. The new companies from the 13th were lettered B, H and K in the new organization. The 30th remained at Winchester until April 10, 1865, when it went to Washington, where it participated in the grand review of the Army of the Potomac on May 23, and on June 2 was transferred to the 2nd brigade, 1st division, 19th corps, which it accompanied to Savannah, Ga., the place of their muster out. On Aug. 24 it arrived in Portland, where the men were finally paid and discharged.

THIRTY-FIRST INFANTRY

Cols., Thomas Hight, Daniel White; Lieut.-Cols., Thomas Hight, Stephen C. Talbot, Edward L. Getchell; Majs., Stephen C. Talbot, Daniel White, George A. Bolton. This regiment was mustered into the U. S. service at Augusta, from March 1 to April 29, 1864, to serve for three years. The 4th and 6th companies of unassigned infantry, organized at Augusta in Oct., 1864, to serve for one year, were assigned to this regiment as Companies L and M, the 32nd Me. was consolidated with this regiment on Dec. 12, 1864, and the entire regiment was mustered out of service near Alexandria, Va. July 15, 1865. The men returned to Bangor on the 19th of the same month, where they were finally paid and discharged on the 27th. The 31st left the state for Washington April 18, 1864, and upon its arrival at Alexandria, Va., was assigned to the 2nd brigade, 2nd division, 9th corps. It at once marched to Bristoe Station, whence it was hastened to the front to aid in the concluding scenes of the conflict. The regiment almost immediately took part in the battle of the Wilderness, where it lost heavily in killed and wounded. From this time on it saw continuous hard service until the close of the war. In addition to the Wilderness it participated in the battles of Spottsylvania Court House, Cold Harbor, Petersburg, Weldon railroad, Poplar Spring Church and Hatcher's run. For its gallantry at the furious engagement of Bethesda Church on June 3, Gen. Griffin, commanding the brigade, issued the following congratulatory order: "It also gives me pleasure to add my evidence to the well-known fact that the 31st Me. has made for itself a most brilliant record, and won for itself imperishable renown." The casualties of the regiment were enormous, as it was so constantly engaged. It lost at Spottsylvania Court House 12 killed, 75 wounded and 108 missing. In the great battle of July 30, when the mine was exploded at Petersburg, the regiment was assigned an important position and was the first to enter the enemy's works. Its losses were 10 killed, 31 wounded and 47 captured. Again at the battle of Poplar Spring Church the regiment distinguished itself, and was the last to fall back when the enemy turned the right of the brigade and compelled a retreat. It lost here 5 killed, 15 wounded and 16 captured. During the winter of 1864-65 it garrisoned Forts Fisher and Davis until Feb. 11, when it was ordered to a point near Parke Station on the Army Line & City Point railroad, where it remained until April 2, when it assaulted the enemy's works and suffered severely. On the next day it participated in the pursuit of the enemy and on the 8th conducted a detachment of prisoners to Ford's station. On the 20th it embarked for Alexandria, Va., and was mustered out the following July.

THIRTY-SECOND INFANTRY

Col., Mark F. Wentworth; Lieut.-Cols., John M. Brown, James L. Hunt; Maj., Arthur Deering. This regiment was raised in the counties of Androscoggin, Cumberland, Franklin, Lincoln, Oxford, Sagadahoc and York, and was mustered in at Augusta, from March 3 to May 6, 1864, to serve for three years. Such was the urgent demand for troops in the field, that six companies which had completed their organization left the state on April 20 for Washington, under the command of Maj. Deering. A few days later they were assigned to the 2nd brigade, 2nd division, 9th corps, and at once hurried to the front. They overtook their corps, which had preceded them by three days, on May 6, and were continuously under fire during the battle of the Wilderness, while engaged in building fortifications and changing position. At Spottsylvania Court House, they were under fire for eight days and rendered most effective service throughout the whole action, holding an exposed part of the line and making numerous charges, losing heavily in men and officers. On the 25th they crossed the North Anna river under fire, and on the 26th were joined by the remaining four companies of the regiment, which had completed their organization on May 6th, and left for the front on the 11th. The following is a list of battles in which this regiment, or a portion of it, bore an honorable part: Spottsylvania Court House, North Anna, Cold Harbor, Petersburg, June 17 to July 30; Weldon railroad, Poplar Spring Church, Pegram farm and Hatcher's run. The regiment charged most gallantly on July 30, when the Confederate works in their immediate front were blown up by Burnside's mine, and was one of the first to enter the works. It came out of this sanguinary fight with but 27 men under Adjt. Hayes, the only officer left, the loss in this engagement being 11 officers and about 100 men killed, wounded and captured. It again met with fearful loss when it sharply engaged the enemy near the Pegram house on Sept. 30. The regiment remained at the Pegram house from Oct. 28 to Nov. 30, and then moved to near Fort Hayes, where it remained until Dec. 12, where, under orders from the war department, 15 of its officers and 470 enlisted men were consolidated with the 31st Me., on account of the reduced state of both regiments, and all surplus officers of the 32nd were mustered out.

FIRST CAVALRY

Cols., John Goddard, Samuel H. Allen, Calvin S. Douty, Charles H. Smith; Lieut.-Cols., Thomas Hight, Calvin S. Douty, Charles H. Smith, Stephen Boothby, Jonathan P. Cilley; Majs., Samuel H. Allen, David P. Stowell, Calvin S. Douty, Warren L. Whitney, Jonathan P. Cilley, Charles H. Smith, Stephen Boothby, George M. Brown, Sidney W. Thaxter, Constantine Taylor, Benjamin F. Tucker, Paul Chadbourne, Daniel S. Curtis, Joel W.

Cloudman. This regiment was raised at large, consisted of twelve companies, and was mustered in at Augusta, Nov. 5, 1861, for three years. It was the equal of any in the service in the character of its men and the quality of its horses. It remained encamped at Augusta until the following spring. Companies A, D, E and F left the state for Washington on March 14, 1862, under command of Col. Allen, arriving there on the 19th. Companies B, I, H and M, under Maj. Douty, arrived on the 24th, and C, G, K and L, under Maj. Stowell, on the 28th. A B, E, H and M, under Lieut.-Col. Douty, joined Gen. Banks' corps at Strasburg, Va., on May 11, and were attached to Gen. Hatch's cavalry brigade. The other seven companies were first assigned to Gen. Abercrombie's brigade, and soon afterwards to Gen. Ord's division at Fredericksburg. The men participated in their first severe engagement on May 23, when Lieut.-Col. Douty with his command and two companies of the 1st Vt. cavalry, charged the enemy at Middletown, Va., covering Banks' retreat to Williamsport. The loss was 176 horses and equipments. The regiment was reunited at Warrenton, Va., on July 10, and attached to Bayard's brigade, with which it took part in the battle of Cedar mountain. It participated in the retreat of Gen. Pope's forces to Fairfax Court House, where it arrived on Sept. 3 and reported to Gen. Reno, having engaged the enemy at Brandy Station on Aug. 20, and been present at the second battle of Bull Run on the 30th, under Brig.-Gen. Elliott of Pope's staff. Arriving in Washington on Sept. 4, it was attached to Burnside's corps and engaged the enemy at Frederick, Md., on the 12th. Co. G, acting as Gen. Reno's bodyguard, took part in the battle of South mountain, Cos. M and H, under Gen. Porter, in that of Antietam. The regiment (except Cos. G, M and H) remained at Frederick from Sept. 12 to Nov. 2, up to which period it had lost in action and worn out in service nearly 700 horses. The severity of the service to which the men of this regiment were subjected may be inferred from a bare recital of the battles in which they were subsequently engaged and from data showing some of their heaviest losses. The list of battles includes, in addition to those above mentioned: Fredericksburg, Rappahannock Station, Brandy Station, Aldie, Middleburg, Upperville, Gettysburg, Shepherdstown, Sulphur Springs, Mine Run, about Richmond, Old Church, Todd's tavern, Ground Squirrel Church, Hawes' shop, Cold Harbor, Trevilian Station, St. Mary's Church, Deep Bottom, Reams' Station, Wyatt's farm,

Boydton road and Bellefield. Col. Douty was killed at Aldie, Va., while leading a gallant charge, on June 17, 1863, as was Capt. Summatt while rallying his men under a murderous fire of grape and canister. Three hundred selected men from the regiment participated in the daring raid of Gen. Kilpatrick to the vicinity of Richmond, Feb. 27 to March 12, 1864, the loss of the 1st in this famous raid being 93 men killed, wounded or missing and over 200 horses. It also moved with the cavalry corps on Gen. Sheridan's first raid, May 9, 1864, until within 3 miles of Richmond. In the engagement at Trevilian Station, June 24, 1864, its loss was 10 officers and 58 enlisted men. During August of this year its loss in killed, wounded and missing was 49 men and 75 horses, and the total casualties during 1864 amounted to 295 officers and enlisted men. In Aug., 1864, seven companies of the 1st D. C. cavalry were transient and assigned to the several companies of this regiment by a special order of the war department. The original members of the regiment whose term of service expired Nov. 4, 1864 were mustered out at Augusta, Me., on the 25th, while the regiment, now composed of veterans, recruits and members of the 1st D. C. cavalry whose term had not expired, participated in the closing battles of the war; was mustered out of the U. S. service at Petersburg, Va., Aug., 1, 1865, and arrived in Augusta, Me., on the 9th.

SECOND CAVALRY

Col., Ephraim W. Woodman; Lieut-Cols., John F. Godfrey, Andrew B. Spurling; Majs., Charles A. Miller, Eben Hutchinson, Andrew B. Spurling, Nathan Cutler. This regiment was organized at Augusta at the close of the year 1863, and the men were mustered in between Nov. 30 and Jan. 2, 1864, to serve for three years. It numbered 989 men, all of good physique and well armed and disciplined. It was assigned to the Department of the Gulf and arrived in five detachments at New Orleans, during April, 1864. Companies A and D, and a part of G, the first to arrive, were at once ordered to Alexandria, La., and assigned to the 3d cavalry brigade, to participate in the Red River expedition. They took part in the engagements at Cherryville cross-roads, Marksville, Avoyelles prairie and Yellow bayou, and rejoined the main body of the regiment at Thibodeaux on June 1. In August the regiment went to Pensacola, Fla., arriving on the 11th, and encamped near Barrancas. During the balance of this year it was engaged in fatigue duty, and participated in raids to Marianna, Fla., and Pollard, Ala. In each of these raids severe damage was inflicted on the enemy, many prisoners and large quantities of stores being captured. In the raid to Pollard four distinct battles were fought, but Lieut.-Col. Spurling, on whom the command of the expedition had devolved, succeeded in conducting his command, encumbered with a train of 50 wagons, 60 miles through the enemy's country, attacked constantly on front, rear and flanks by a superior force. The regiment suffered much during the summer of 1864, from sickness, induced by a sudden change to the excessive heat of southern Louisiana. At one time only 450 were able to report for duty, and during the year the regiment lost by deaths one officer and 278 enlisted men. On Feb. 23, 1865, Lieut.-Col. Spurling with 300 men routed the enemy at Milton, Fla. The regiment joined Gen. Steele's command at Pensacola on March 19, and participated in the campaign which resulted in the capture of Mobile, and opened up the State of Alabama to the Union forces. The regiment rendered highly efficient service, captured many prisoners, destroyed much railroad and other property, frequently engaged the enemy, and opened communication with Gen. Canby, who was besieging Spanish Fort. After the fall of Mobile, a detachment of the regiment accompanied the 16th corps on a 200-mile march to Montgomery, Ala. In Aug., 1865, detachments of the regiment were stationed at various points in western Florida to preserve the peace. On Dec. 1, it was concentrated at Barrancas, and was mustered out on the 6th, though 25 officers and 116 men remained in Florida, and 14 officers and 500 enlisted men returned to Augusta, where they were finally paid and discharged.

FIRST DISTRICT OF COLUMBIA CAVALRY

This regiment, known as Baker's cavalry, was an independent organization and was originally designed for special service in the District of Columbia, subject only to the orders of the war department. It was commanded by Col. L. C. Baker. Eight companies were organized at Augusta, from Oct., 1863, to March, 1864, to serve for three years, and assigned as Cos. D, F, G, H, I,

K, L and M, rendering the regiment to all intents and purposes a Maine organization. Capt. Cloudman, whose company was the first to leave the state for Washington, was commissioned major by the president, during the seven months' service of the regiment, which was engaged in important service in and about Washington until May, when half of it was ordered to Portsmouth, Va., and dismounted for a short time. The other half was assigned to the army of Gen. Butler and participated in Gen. Kautz' cavalry raids about Petersburg, in May and June, 1864. In July this portion participated in the engagement at Malvern hill, and Aug. crossed the Appomattox river and established headquarters at Sycamore Church, with four companies stationed at Cox's mills, 2 miles below. The regiment was engaged in skirmishing and doing picket duty on the Weldon & Petersburg railroad, Aug. 8-23, and on the latter date engaged and drove the Hampton legion, inflicting a severe loss on the enemy. On the 24th, it took part in the action at Reams' station, after which it returned to Sycamore Church, and on the 27th, by a special order of the war department, all the Maine officers and men were transferred to the 1st Me. cavalry. They did not join the latter regiment at once, but remained doing duty on the extreme left of the army, on a line about 4 miles in length. On Sept. 15, the regiment was attacked simultaneously at three points on their extended line by an overwhelming force of the enemy, and after a heroic resistance was compelled to retreat. The loss was severe, 9 officers and over 150 privates being captured, in addition to several killed and wounded. Majs. Baker and Cloudman were captured, and the remaining men then joined the 1st Me. cavalry, their history from this date being identical with that regiment.

FIRST HEAVY ARTILLERY

Cols., Daniel Chaplin, Russell B. Shepherd; Lieut.-Cols., Thomas H. Talbot, Russell B. Shepherd, Zemro A. Smith; Majs., Charles Hamlin, Russell B. Shepherd, George W. Sabine, Christopher V. Crossman, Zemro A. Smith, Charles W. Nute, Harrison G. Smith. This regiment was originally organized as the 18th infantry (q. v.), but was changed to heavy artillery after five months' service, and by general order No. 62, from the adjutant-general's office of Maine, series of 1862, was designated as the 1st regiment, heavy artillery, Maine volunteers. Two additional companies were organized—one in Jan., 1864, the other in Feb., 1864. The original members were mustered out on June 6, 1865, but the organization, composed of veterans and recruits of this regiment and accessions from the 17th and 19th Me. infantry, remained in service and was mustered out at Washington, D. C., Sept. 11, 1865. The men returned to Bangor, Me., on the 17th and were paid and discharged on the 20th. The several companies were stationed in the defenses of Washington until 1864. The 3d battery of mounted artillery was temporarily attached to this regiment, and served as Co. M, from March 28, 1863, to Feb. 23, 1864. The maximum number of men required for the regiment (1,800), was secured in Feb., 1864, when two new majors were added and four lieutenants in each company instead of two. On May 15, 1864, the regiment as thus organized joined the Army of the Potomac at Belle Plain landing and came under fire for the first time on the 19th, when it took a prominent part in repulsing a heavy attack of the enemy on the supply trains near the Fredericksburg pike. It suffered severely in the action, losing 476 men in killed, wounded and missing. It subsequently participated in the battles of Totopotomy, Cold Harbor, Petersburg, Deep Bottom, Boydton road, Weldon railroad, Hatcher's run, and in all the final movements resulting in the evacuation of Richmond and Petersburg and the surrender of Gen. Lee. On May 24, 1864, the regiment was assigned to the 3d brigade, 3d division, 2nd corps. In the heroic assaults on the enemy's works at Petersburg, between June 15-30, the regiment lost 30 killed 519 wounded, and 31 missing, 6 of the killed being commissioned officers. Col. Chaplin was mortally wounded by a sharpshooter on Aug. 18 at Deep Bottom, and in the action on the Boydton plank road, Oct. 27, the regiment lost 3 commissioned officers and 29 men. In an engagement of a little more than an hour at Hatcher's run, March 25, 1865, it lost 1 officer and 3 men killed, and 23 wounded and captured. The regiment was at Bailey's cross-roads April 16, and later participated in the grand review at Washington.

Col., Freeman McGilvery; Lieut-Cols., Davis Tillson, George F. Leppien, Freeman McGilvery, James A. Hall; Majs., Davis Tillson, Freeman McGilvery, James A. Hall, Albert W. Bradbury. This organization was composed of seven batteries, serving in different commands, which were mustered into service for three years. The 1st battery was organized at Portland, Dec. 18, 1861, and mustered out there on July 1, 1865; the 2nd was organized at Augusta, Nov. 30, 1861, and mustered out at the same city on June 6, 1865; the 3d was organized at Augusta, Dec. 11, 1861, and mustered out at Augusta on June 17, 1865; the 4th was organized at Augusta, Dec. 21, 1861, and mustered out there on June 17, 1863; the 5th was organized at Augusta, Dec. 4, 1861, and mustered out at Augusta, July 6, 1865; the 6th was organized at Augusta, Feb. 7, 1862, and mustered out at the same place on June 17, 1865; the 7th was organized at Augusta, Dec. 30, 1863, and mustered out there on June 21, 1865. The 1st battery left the state for Camp Chase, Lowell, Mass., Dec. 19, 1861, and arrived at Ship island, Miss., March 10, 1862. It moved to New Orleans May 15, and did patrol and garrison duty until Oct. 1, when it became a part of Gen. Weitzel's reserve brigade at Carrollton. The battery remained in the South until Feb. 10, 1864, during which period it was in the engagements at Labadieville, Bayou Teche, Fort Bisland, siege of Port Hudson and Donaldsonville. Every man present for duty with the battery reenlisted for three years on Dec. 29, 1863, and was mustered in Jan. 1, following. The men were furloughed for 30 days in Feb. and March, 1864, and the battery was assigned to Gen. Burnside's corps in April. On July 12 it assisted in repelling Gen. Early's forces at Fort Stevens. On the 30th it was assigned to the 19th corps, Gen. Emory commanding, and joined the 1st division on Aug. 3. It remained with this division through the balance of the year, participating in the brilliant campaign of Gen. Sheridan in the Shenandoah valley. It was in the actions at Winchester, Strasburg and Cedar creek, in all of which it distinguished itself. On Nov. 9 it moved from Cedar creek to Winchester, and Jan. 14 to Manchester. On April 14 returned to Winchester and on July 9 embarked for Portland.

The 2nd battery garrisoned Fort Preble from March 10 to April 1, 1862, when it left for Washington. It participated in the action at Cross Keys, June 8, and in skirmishes at Strasburg, Woodstock, Mount Jackson, Newmarket, Harrisonburg and Port Republic. On Aug. 5, it moved from Waterloo to Culpeper Court House and engaged the enemy near there on the 8th. It was also engaged in the second Bull Run, the battle of Cedar mountain, and was in the battle of Fredericksburg, Dec. 13, losing 2 killed and 14 wounded, and 31 horses. It then encamped at Fletcher's Chapel until May 3, 1863, when it engaged in the battle of Chancellorsville, after which it took part in the Pennsylvania campaign, and in the battle of Gettysburg. In Dec., 1863, most of the men reenlisted for three years, and were given furloughs of 30 days. The battery was at Camp Barry until April 26, 1864, and was then assigned to the 9th corps, Army of the Potomac, taking part in the advance on Richmond and the battles of the Wilderness, Spottsylvania Court House (eight days' fighting), North Anna, Bethesda Church, Cold Harbor and Petersburg. From Oct. 13, 1864, to May 3, 1865, it occupied the outer defenses of City Point, Va., when it moved to Alexandria, and on May 31 left there for Maine.

The 3d battery remained in barracks at Island Park, Portland, until April 1, 1862, when it left for Washington. It served with Gen. McDowell as pontoniers from May 14 to Nov. 7; was then engaged in building battery "Maine" at Fort Lincoln until March 28, 1863, when it was assigned to the 1st Me. heavy artillery as Co. M, and remained in the defenses of Washington as part of that organization until it was reorganized on Feb. 22, 1864. Meanwhile, 72 of the men had reenlisted for three years, on Jan. 5, 1864, and returned home on a 30-days' furlough. The reorganized battery remained at Camp Barry, Washington, until July 5 when it moved to City Point, Va., and was assigned to the 3d division, 9th corps, then before Petersburg. It remained in the trenches before Petersburg from July 9 to Oct. 25, with three days exception, and was then in the defenses of City Point until May 3, 1865, when it went to Washington and left there for Maine on June 2.

The 4th battery remained at Portland until April 1, 1862, when it left for Washington. It was stationed in and about Washington until June 28, when it joined Gen. Sigel's command in their march up the Shenandoah valley and participated in the battle of Cedar mountain, losing 1 killed, 6 wounded and 1 missing. Later it returned to Culpeper with Gen. Banks' corps, and retreated to Washington with Gen. Pope's army. It was in the battle of Antietam, and spent the winter of 1862-63 at Shepherdstown and Harper's Ferry. After the defeat of Gen. Milroy at Winchester, it moved to Monocacy Junction, and on July 8 was assigned to the 3d corps, Gen. French commanding. It was engaged in the action at Wapping heights, Oct. 15, and at Kelly's ford, Nov. 7, and went into camp at Brandy Station on the 11th. It was engaged on Nov. 30 at Mine Run, returned to Brandy Station and remained there until March 31, 1864, where it was assigned to the artillery brigade of the 6th corps and participated in the battle of Cold Harbor. From June 17 to July 13, 1864, it was in position in front of Petersburg and was then ordered to join the 6th corps at Washington. Finding the corps advanced to Harper's Ferry, the battery returned to Petersburg, and was assigned temporarily to the 8th corps. It was in the action of July 30, losing 2 men. On Dec. 21, 1864, 21 of the original members were mustered out, but the battery remained in service until June 17, 1865.

The 5th battery left for Washington April 1, 1862. On May 19 it marched to Fredericksburg, thence to Front Royal and Cedar mountain, where it took position under a heavy artillery fire. On Aug. 20 it moved to Rappahannock Station and covered the railroad crossing. It retreated with the army on Aug. 23, participating in the engagements at Thoroughfare gap, and at Manassas, where 4 of the guns were captured after the battery was deserted by its infantry supports. The battery then refitted at Washington, rejoined its division and took part in the battle of Fredericksburg, being highly complimented there for accuracy of aim and rapidity of fire. It wintered at Fletcher's Chapel until April 28, 1863, and on May 2 suffered severely in the battle of Chancellorsville, losing 31 men killed and wounded and 40 horses killed and disabled. It was in winter quarters at Culpeper from Dec. 24 1863, to April 15, 1864, when it was placed in the reserve corps and encamped at Rappahannock Station. It moved with the reserves to the Wilderness and Spottsylvania, and on May 17, 1864, was permanently assigned to the 6th corps. On June 2 it silenced the enemy's batteries in their front at Cold Harbor, and on the 18th moved to Petersburg, where it engaged the enemy on the 21st. Later it took part in the defensive operations of the 6th corps at Washington. On Sept. 30, at Harrisonburg,

Va., one section of battery A, 1st Mass., was assigned to this battery. It was heavily engaged at the battle of Cedar creek, Oct. 19, 1864, where it lost 29 men and 31 horses; was at Winchester, Nov. 1; moved to Frederick on Jan. 10, 1865; returned to Winchester on April 4, and on June 21 was ordered to Maine.

The 6th battery left for Washington March 21, 1862, and served under Gens. Sigel, Banks and Heintzelman in Virginia, and Gens. Williams and Slocum in Maryland. It was engaged at Cedar mountain, losing 13 men; took part in all the fighting on the Rappahannock under Gen. Pope, and at the battles of Centerville and Manassas lost 13 men. The battery was assigned to the 1st brigade, 2nd division, 12th corps, and remained at Dumfries, Va., from Dec., 1862, to May 27, 1863, when it was assigned to the reserve corps at Falmouth. It took a prominent part in the battle of Gettysburg and in the skirmishes of the 1st corps on the retreat from Culpeper. It was at Brandy Station from Dec. 3 to April 22, 1864. Meanwhile, more than two-thirds of the men had reenlisted for three years. The battery took part in the advance of the Army of the Potomac to Richmond, and saw much hard service during the campaign, participating in the battles of the Wilderness, Spottsylvania, Cold Harbor, Petersburg, Opequan, Fisher's hill and Cedar creek.

The 7th battery left for Washington Feb. 1, 1864, and joined the 9th corps on April 25. It joined in the advance on Richmond and was engaged in the battles of the Wilderness, Spottsylvania Court House, North Anna, Cold Harbor, Petersburg, Reams' station and Poplar Spring Church. It held a position near the Taylor house, immediately in front of and 700 yards from the point where the mine was sprung on July 30, 1864, for 47 consecutive days. From Dec, 2, 1864, to April 1, 1865, it occupied Fort Sedgwick and participated in the general assault resulting in the capture of Petersburg. It returned to Washington April 20; was in the grand review, May 23, and on June 5 left for Maine.

COMPANY D, SECOND U.S. SHARPSHOOTERS

This company was organized at Augusta, Nov. 2, 1861, to serve for three years. The secretary of war had requested the governor to contribute a company of rifle sharpshooters to the general government and the men were selected with great care. James

D. Fessenden of Portland superintended the formation of the company, and went out as captain. It left the state for Washington Nov. 13, 1861, and was assigned to Col. Berdan's regiment, the 2nd U. S. sharpshooters, until Feb. 18, 1865, when the surviving reenlisted members thereof were transferred to the 17th Me. infantry (q. v.). During its term of service it shared in many important battles and skirmishes, including the second Bull Run, Antietam, Fredericksburg, Chancellorsville, Gettysburg and all the battles of the final campaign of the Army of the Potomac in 1864.

FIRST SHARPSHOOTERS

Lieut.-Col., Jacob McClure. This regiment was composed of six companies, and was organized at Augusta, from Oct. 27 to Dec. 29, 1864, to serve one and three years, and was consolidated with the 20th Me. infantry, June 21, 1865. Cos. A and B left for the front Nov. 12, 1864, and were assigned to the defenses at City Point, Va. Cos. C, D, E and F left Augusta on Dec. 7 and Dec. 30 and proceeded to Galloupe's island in Boston harbor, where they remained until Jan. 1, 1865, when they were ordered to City Point. They joined the two companies already there on the 5th, and remained until the 21st, when the war department decided there was no authority for such a regiment. The lieutenant-colonel commanding was mustered out of service, the command was ordered to report to the 5th army corps and joined the 20th Me. infantry on June 21.

COAST GUARD ARTILLERY

This organization, composed of three companies (A, B and C), commenced to organize in July, 1861, to serve for three years as garrison artillery in the state. This was the more necessary as most of the efficient, active militia of the state had already been absorbed into the U. S. service and left the state. The above companies were stationed as follows: Co. A, Capt. Ira Andrews, at Fort McClary, Kittery, relieving Capt. M. F. Wentworth's company of artillery, which had been doing duty since April 30, 1861; Co. B, Capt. James Staples, Fort Scammel Portland harbor; Co.

C, composed of a detachment of 40 men under Lieut. George W. Sabine, at Fort Sullivan, Eastport. They occupied these several stations until Sept. 13, 1862, when they were mustered out of service in accordance with orders from the war department.

FIRST INFANTRY BATTALION

This organization was composed of the 21st, 24th, 25th and 26th companies of unassigned infantry and was mustered into the U. S. service at Augusta, in Feb. and March, 1865, to serve for one year. It was designed for the 15th Me. infantry, but was organized as the 1st battalion on May 25, 1865, as there was no vacancy in the 15th. The companies were lettered A, B, C and D, and were assigned to the 2nd brigade, Dwight's division, then in the Shenandoah valley, and subsequently moved to Washington, where it remained until June 1. From there it moved to Savannah, Ga., and on July 6 was ordered to South Carolina, where it did duty at various places until April 5, 1866, when it was mustered out at Charleston, S. C.

UNASSIGNED COMPANIES

Thirty unassigned companies of infantry were organized at Augusta during the closing months of 1864 and in the early months of 1865, to serve for one, two and three years, of which twenty-three were assigned to different regiments of Maine infantry in the field. The 27th and 28th companies were never mustered finally into the U. S. service; the 7th was assigned to garrison Fort Popham, on the Maine coast; the 9th was attached to the engineer brigade, Army of the James; and the 19th, 20th and 30th remained at Augusta.

COAST GUARD BATTALION

This organization was composed of seven companies of infantry, and was mustered into the U. S. service at Belfast, Augusta and Eastport from March 18, 1864, to March 2, 1865, to serve for one, two and three years. Co. A, mustered in at Belfast, March

18, 1864, for three years, left for Washington on May 2, and was assigned to garrison Fort Washington, Md. It was mustered out at Portland, Me., May 25, 1865. Co. B, mustered in at Augusta, April 27, 1864, to serve for three years, left Rockland May 5, 1864, for Washington, and was stationed at Fort Foote, Md. It was mustered out at Portland, Me., June 24, 1865. Co. C, mustered in at Eastport, May 16,1864, to serve for three years, was stationed at Fort Sullivan, Me., and was mustered out at Portland, Sept. 6, 1865. Co. D, mustered in at Augusta, Jan. 6, 1865, to serve for one, two and three years, was stationed at Machiasport, Me., and was mustered out Sept. 6, 1865, at Portland. Co. E, mustered in at Augusta, Jan. 7, 1865, to serve for one, two and three years, was stationed at Rockland, and was mustered out July 7, 1865. Co. F, mustered in at Augusta, Jan. 6, 1865, to serve for one year, was stationed at Belfast, Me., and was mustered out July 7, 1865. Co. G, mustered in March 1, 1865, was stationed first at Augusta, and afterwards at Calais, Me. It was mustered out at Augusta, July 6, 1865.

MILITIA COMPANIES

Three militia companies were mustered into the U. S. service in 1864, to garrison the forts on the Maine coast; Co. A. 1st State Guards, was mustered in at Bangor, July 7, 1864 and mustered out at Bangor, Sept. 8, 1864, after being stationed for 60 days at Fort McClary, Kittery, Me. Co. B, 1st State Guards, was mustered in at Bangor, to serve for 60 days, and was stationed at Fort McClary. It was mustered out at Bangor, Nov. 7, 1864. Co. H, 1st regiment light infantry, was consolidated with a detachment of Co. G, same regiment and mustered into the U. S. service at Fort McClary, April 27, 1864, to serve for 60 days. It was mustered out July 9, 1864, at Portland.

INDEX

79

82

84

85

88

89

Walker, Charles 40
Walker, Elijah 33
Wapping Heights, VA
  Battle of 71
Warren, Gouverneur K. 50
Warrenton, VA 64
Warsaw Island, GA 39
Wartrace, TN 41
Warwick Creek, VA 36, 42
Washburn, Israel, Jr. 7, 9, 10, 11,
  14, 17
Washington 24
Washington Arsenal 60
Washington, DC 3, 5, 9, 11, 17,
  18, 21, 24, 29, 32, 33, 34, 35,
  36, 37, 39, 41, 42, 48, 49, 50,
  51, 52, 53, 54, 55, 56, 57, 58,
  61, 62, 64, 66, 67, 68, 70, 71,
  72, 73, 74, 75
Washington Relief Association 24
Waterloo, VA 70
Waterville, ME 32
Webber, _____ 18
Weitzel, Godfrey 69
Welch, James W. 51
Weldon & Petersburg Railroad 67
Weldon Railroad, VA
  Battle of 37, 49, 50, 52, 62, 63,
  68
Wentworth, M. F. 73
Wentworth, Mark F. 57, 62
West, George W. 49
West Point, VA
  Battle of 34
Westbrook, ME 29
White, Daniel 31, 61
White Oak Bridge, VA
  Battle of 35
White Oak Church, VA 36
White Oak Road, VA
  Battle of 2
White Oak Swamp, VA
  Battle of 33, 36, 42
Whiting Military Academy 1
Whitman, Royal E. 61

Whitmore, James H. 47
Whitney, Warren L. 63
Wilderness, VA
  Battle of 33, 34, 35, 37, 49, 50,
  51, 52, 62, 63, 70, 71, 72
Wildes, Asa W. 48
Williams, Reuel 11
Williamsburg, VA
  Battle of 33, 35, 36, 42
Williamsport, MD 40, 64
Wilmington, NC 39
Winchester, VA 40, 61, 69, 72
  Battle of 14, 44, 46
  Battle of (1863) 71
  Battle of (1864) 59, 60, 69
Winterport, ME 9
Wiscasset, ME 12
Wisconsin Units
  Infantry
    4th Wisconsin 40
Wiswell, Joseph M. 46
Witham, Albion 29
Woodman, Ephraim W. 37, 58, 65
Woodstock, ME 9
Woodstock, VA 70
Wyatt's Farm, VA
  Battle of 64

Y

Yellow Bayou, LA
  Engagement at 65
York County, ME 49, 57, 62
Yorktown, VA 35, 36, 42
  Battle of 30, 42
  Siege of 35, 36

Z

Zina H. Robinson 38

OTHER PAPERBACK TITLES FROM
eBooksOnDisk

Civil War Regiments from Wisconsin by Jerome A. Watrous.
ISBN 1932157115

Civil War Regiments from New Jersey by James Stewert, Jr.
ISBN 1932157239

Civil War Regiments from Massachusetts by Francis
Agustus Osborn
ISBN 1932157212

Confederate Military History of Alabama by Joseph Wheeler.
ISBN 1932157174

Confederate Military History of Florida by J. J. Dickison.
ISBN 1932157093

Confederate Military History of Mississippi by Charles E.
Hooker.
ISBN 1932157182

Confederate Military History of Texas by Oran M. Robert.
ISBN 193215714X

Regimental Losses in the American Civil War by William F. Fox
1932157077

Printed in the United States
50568LVS00004B/268

9 781932 157246